100-Minute Buddha

Jinananda

The 100-Minute Press, Canterbury

Publisher

The 100-Minute Press Ltd.
Mystole Farm
Canterbury, Kent, CT4 7DB
United Kingdom

Title: The 100-Minute Buddha

Author

Jinananda

First Edition 2010
ISBN 978-09556695-1-4

Copyright © Jinananda 2010

The use of short portions of this publication, i.e. up to one section, is permitted without reference to the Publisher. The publisher requests that the origin of such extracts should be acknowledged as *The 100-Minute Buddha*.
A copyright licence is available to Communities and Sanghas. For details contact sales@the100-minutepress.com.

Printed by PB Group Ltd, Sittingbourne, Kent, UK

Cover: Jason Etienne

Contents

Chapter		Page No
Preface		i
1.	Birth: this precious human life	2
2.	The legend of the four sights	4
3.	Renunciation: the seeker after truth	6
4.	Awakening	8
5.	Compassion: Siddartha becomes the Buddha	10
6.	The Four Noble Truths	12
7.	The Noble Eightfold Path	14
8.	The story of the gilt slippers	16
9.	An organisation of compassion	18
10.	Delusion: the matted haired fire-worshippers	20
11.	Attachment: the Fire Sermon	22
12.	The Buddha confronts Nihilism	24
13.	Nanda and the path of bliss	26
14.	Reflection: the Buddha teaches his son	28
15.	Giving: the world's first monastery	30
16.	The admission of women into the Order	32
17.	Friendship: the Buddha's attendants	34
18.	The Buddha's guide to ordinary happiness	36
19.	Patience. The story of Sundari	38
20.	Abandoning violence: 'Finger-necklace', the serial killer	40
21.	Shame and ethics	42
22.	Confession and the ocean of the Dharma	44
23.	Understanding the Dharma: 3 parables	46
24.	Religious disputes: the blind men and the elephant	48
25.	Miracles: The Buddha and God	50

26.	Karma	52
27.	What is reborn?	54
28.	Impermanence	56
29.	How do you know what to believe in?	58
30.	Self-reliance and mind-training	60
31.	Balancing energy: Sona and his guitar	62
32.	Patience and guarding the mind	64
33.	Mindfulness	66
34.	Meditation: distractions and concentration	68
35.	The cultivation of loving-kindness	70
36.	Measuring attainment: the ten fetters	72
37.	The nature of Enlightenment	74
38.	The Awakening and death of Bahia	76
39.	Caring for the sick and dying	78
40.	Pingiya's faith	80
41.	Devadatta: the great betrayer	82
42.	The fruits of the Buddhist life	84
43.	The Buddha's farewell to life	86
44.	The passing of the Buddha	88
45.	The Buddha's funeral and the first Council	90
46.	The Lotus Sutra	92
47.	The Lotus Sutra: parables and prophecies	94
48.	The Happy Land Sutra	96
49.	Amitabha's vows	98
50.	The Diamond Sutra	100

Preface

Buddhism, known to Buddhists as the Buddha Dharma, or simply the Dharma, is clearly a religion, with its own rituals, worship, monks, robes, hierarchies and inevitable doctrinal spats. However, before launching into its literature it may be helpful to dispel certain assumptions that tend to gather around religious narratives but that do not apply in the case of Buddhism. Various conventions of Buddhist discourse that may ring oddly to people brought up in a Judaeo-Christian or Muslim culture arise from a profoundly different way of seeing things.

Firstly, Buddhist cosmology or creation myths are of little importance. There is certainly no creator god in Buddhism. Nor is there an absence or rejection of such a being, as might be experienced by, say, an atheist. There is no God-shaped hole. For a Buddhist the very idea that one has been put into this world could never arise. One is encouraged to take responsibility for one's experience of life as far as one can for the very practical reason that this also gives one the power to change that experience. In the Buddhist scriptures there is much mention of gods and the 'heaven realms' that such beings live in, but they are part of the scenery along with nature spirits, ogres and so on. The gods are respected as spiritually powerful, but are ultimately limited by comparison with a Buddha.

Secondly the Buddha is a founder and exemplar, not a saviour, and the emphasis of his teachings is on experience and practice rather than belief. Generally speaking, Buddhist faith is based on an experience of the positive results of practising what the Buddha taught. The tone is one of 'try this and see how it works'. Consequently, Buddhism is a system of practice rather than a 'belief system,' and Buddhists are generally known as 'practitioners' rather than 'believers'.

Ethics is seen as a skill to be developed with its own natural rewards, which include avoiding the suffering that naturally follows from being unethical, in future lives as well as the present one. There is therefore no place for a being who rewards or punishes one's ethics; and being unethical becomes simply unintelligent rather than rebellious. Buddhism is also particularly associated with meditation and mindfulness, which amongst other things act as a magnifying glass on the practitioner's mental processes, enabling them to redirect those processes into the most positive channels. These aspects of Buddhist practice have been successfully applied in psychotherapeutic contexts. However, their ultimate function is to enable the practitioner to turn an intellectual understanding of the true nature of things into an embodied experience of it.

Thirdly, the Buddha is not merely a human being. As a Buddha he is free of all the coming and going between the human realm, the heaven realms and the hells. The Buddha is neither man nor God. The goal of Buddhism is not to go to heaven but to achieve what the Buddha achieved. This is strictly speaking inconceivable, but is described in various different ways, as an Awakening to one's true nature, or an Enlightenment or Liberation of the mind, or as nirvana, a 'snuffing out' or extinction of the mental poisons of greed, hatred and delusion. On a cognitive level it is wisdom; on an emotional level it is compassion.

Like other world religions, Buddhism has blossomed into a wide variety of traditions of practice and doctrine. The fact that

Buddhists tolerate doctrinal differences does not mean that these are insignificant. Of the various schools of Tibetan Buddhism, only one is presided over by the Dalai Lama, and they each have their own particular teachings and practices. The Tibetan Buddhist tradition as a whole differs markedly from the Zen schools of Japan, China, Korea and Vietnam, and these in turn take a quite different approach from the Chinese and Japanese Pure Land or devotional schools (which include the largest Buddhist denominations in the world today). Furthermore, all these major branches of Buddhism, which together call themselves the Mahayana, are based around scriptures that the Theravada Buddhists of Sri Lanka and Burma, Thailand and Cambodia, do not regard as having been taught by the Buddha. However, Buddhists of all denominations share a common set of values and a recognisable Buddhist sensibility: a cheerful, kindly demeanour, an open-minded pragmatism, and a strong resistance to being drawn into hatred or violence.

These qualities all derive from the Buddha and his teachings, remembered and preserved orally for several hundred years, before being written down in the first century BC. The most complete surviving collection of these early discourses (known as suttas) was written down in Sri Lanka in the ancient language of Pali. These scriptures on their own will fill a small bookcase. However, if you add the scriptures of the various Mahayana schools, most of which appeared originally in Sanskrit, you would need a small library.

There is no clear narrative continuity or running order through all these volumes. So any selection and arrangement of texts that one might make is inevitably an artificial construct. In the main I have drawn upon the Pali texts (known in English as the Pali canon) in the following pages, because they centre upon the historical Buddha and because most of the teachings they contain are accepted by all schools of Buddhism. I have included the most significant events of the Buddha's own life and the early Buddhist community as well as covering the main themes of his teaching in a selection of the better known stories of his ministry, plus a few less well-known ones. However, I have also included key excerpts from Mahayana texts that express the Buddha's presence and teaching in more archetypal and mythical terms. Traditional Buddhist technical terms appear in the language in which they are most familiar; nirvana for example is the Sanskrit version of the term; but on the other hand I use the Pali word metta for the Buddhist ideal of universal loving-kindness.

Jinananda

West London Buddhist Centre

July 2010

India at the time of the Buddha

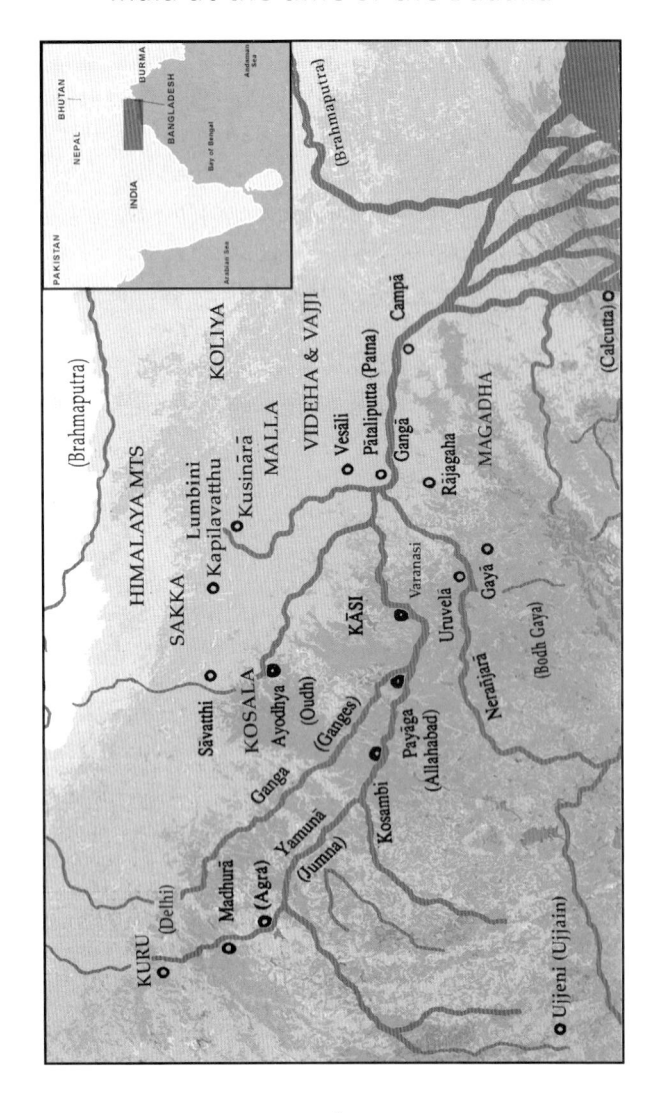

1. Birth: this precious human life

The Buddha was not a god. He was a man who 'woke up', who became a Buddha, 'one who is fully awake,' or one who lives in accordance with how things really are. It is this achievement, his 'Enlightenment', that is the key event in his life.

Only in hindsight, therefore, does his early life take on any significance; and not just because he became Enlightened. Any human being can do the same, with enough effort. The importance of the Buddha is that he was the first. He discovered the way to Enlightenment, called the Dharma, and he founded the Sangha, the community of practitioners who make the path to Awakening available to us today. And even in this he was not unique. He re-discovered the Way. The Dharma has been lost and found many times in legendary ages past, and even though knowledge of it will disappear, as all things must do, the Buddhist faith holds that it will be rediscovered again in the future.

The various traditional accounts of the Buddha's birth and early life are a mixture of myth, legend and history. He was born about 485 BC the son of the elected chieftain of the Sukyan tribal republic, whose territory stood on the current border between India and Nepal. Hence the title he would be given, Sakyamuni, *meaning the Sage of the Sakyans.*

He had resolved to be a Buddha in a previous life, as a disciple of a previous Buddha. This resolution made him a *Bodhisattva*, a being dedicated to Enlightenment, and he was reborn as a god, before his final rebirth as a human being.

On a full moon night Queen Maya dreamt of a great elephant bearing a white lotus, which circled round her bed and struck her side, entering her womb. Dream interpreters said that she would bear a child who would become either an Emperor or a Buddha. When the child was delivered, in the Lumbini gardens near the Sakyan capital of Kapilavastu, a wise man, Asita the Black, learned of it from the gods, and came down from the Himalayas to find him. Beholding him at last, he wept for he saw that the child would be a Buddha, and that he himself would not live to hear his teaching. The boy was named Siddhartha, and his family name was Gotama, of the *ksatriya* or warrior caste. As his mother died in childbirth, he was brought up by his aunt, Mahaprajapati.

Siddartha was not born a Buddha, but something happened in his childhood to set him on the path to Buddhahood.

Nk. SN 3.11

2. The legend of the four sights

Young Siddartha had a privileged upbringing. His father lavished all manner of luxuries on him: silk clothes, rich food and skilled courtesans. In this way he hoped to divert his son from anything that might cause him to reflect on life. He was concerned by predictions that his son might become a Buddha and he wanted him to stay focused on worldly pursuits. So he also had him trained in the military arts, and in due course arranged for him to be married, to a girl called Yasodhara. But at some point awareness broke through the round of work and pleasure.

One day Siddhartha went out with his charioteer, Channa, and as they drove through the streets he was struck by the sight of a decrepit old man. He asked Channa, 'What is the matter with him?' Channa said, 'Old age. It comes to us all.' Siddhartha was thunderstruck, and turned home, distraught. On a second excursion they came upon a sick man. Siddhartha said: 'What is that man doing', and Channa replied, 'He is sick, he cannot help shaking and panting. At some point everyone suffers in that way.' Siddhartha trembled with horror like the moon reflected on ruffled water, and he ordered the chariot home.

A few days later his spirits recovered, and they went out again; this time they came across a dead man. Siddhartha looked at Channa, puzzled. Channa explained that the man's life was finished, and his body would be disposed of, burnt or buried. Hearing this, Siddhartha could take no more pleasure in jaunts and distractions. He did not understand how people could live as if suffering would not touch them, and ignore the suffering of others. He later recalled his thoughts at that time as a turning point:

'I considered how most people feel fearful, humiliated and disgusted when they come across old age, sickness and death in others, forgetting that they are subject to these things themselves... and all the intoxication of youth faded from my heart.'

Finally, on a fourth outing in his chariot, Siddhartha spotted a man in rags carrying a bowl. Channa told him that this man had left home, abandoned the world, and sought liberation from *samsara*, 'the going on and on of things'. He sought an ending to the dissatisfaction of mundane existence that propelled itself from one life to the next in an endless series of rebirths. Siddhartha went home filled with renewed hope.

During this time, whilst he was contemplating old age and death, his wife Yasodhara gave birth to a son, Rahula.

Mv, Lv, Bc, AN 3.38

3. Renunciation: the seeker after truth

In the homeless wanderer Siddhartha saw the possibility of a solution to certain problems of life: ageing, sickness, death, impermanence and suffering: in a word, *samsara*.

'Why do I', he reflected, 'being mortal myself, chase after mortal things? Why don't I seek instead the unborn, the deathless?'

'Domestic life is stifling and dusty; the going forth as a wanderer is free and open. It is not easy to live the completely authentic life, beautiful like a sea shell, while hemmed in at home.'

The legends tell how Siddhartha, with a last lingering look at his sleeping wife and child, slipped out of the palace accompanied by Channa holding onto his horse's tail, and of how the gods muffled his hoof-beats and silently opened the city gates. Arriving at the River Anoma he cut off his hair and said good-bye to Channa and his horse. A little later he surrendered his silk clothes to a passing huntsman, accepting his rough clothing in exchange. He headed for Vaisali, and soon found a teacher, Alara Kalama.

Siddhartha quickly attained the meditative goal set before him, a vibrant emptiness of mental objects. But he found that when he emerged from this concentration, compulsive negative thoughts would soon return. So he and his friends moved on to another teacher, Uddaka Ramaputta, who taught a further attainment, that of neither perception nor non-perception. But again, it relied on the conditions being in place that would support meditative concentration. It was impermanent.

In their travels, Siddhartha met Bimbisara, King of Magadha, who offered him a position of political power. But he turned it down. He had one more path to explore. He settled near Uruvela, at a place now called Bodhgaya, to practise austerities, to burn away the mind's impurities with self-inflicted hardship. He was joined in his endeavours by five other seekers, inspired by his single-minded commitment.

Siddhartha practised holding his breath until it felt 'as if a strap were being twisted round my head, as if a butcher were cutting through my body, as if I were being held over hot coals'. Then he starved himself: 'my limbs became like vine-stems, my spine like a row of spindles, my ribs like the rafters of an uncovered barn, and my eyes like the gleam of water at the bottom of a well.'

In a few years Siddhartha was famed throughout the region as a holy man. Austerities are still practised in India today – but they form no part of Buddhism, because Siddartha eventually saw that he had attained nothing by them.

SN: 3.2. DN ii 21. Mv. MN 36

4. Awakening

Siddhartha was in his early thirties, and still at Bodhgaya, when he finally gave up the path of asceticism, as a result of remembering an event from his childhood which seemed to offer a radical alternative. As a young boy he had been sitting under a rose-apple tree watching his father ploughing and had fallen into a natural and joyful state of concentration. He now thought,

'Why be afraid of pleasure and happiness? So long as it does not take control of the mind and lead to craving, perhaps this is the way.'

So he broke his fast and enjoyed his food. His five companions, who had been relying on him to lead them to the goal of liberation from sense desires, left him in disgust.

He bathed in the nearby River Neranjara. Afterwards, a woman called Sujata brought rice milk as an offering to the god of the banyan tree he was sitting under, and mistaking him for the god, gave it to him. Having eaten, and facing east, he resolved: 'Flesh and blood may dry up, but without attaining Enlightenment I will not leave this seat.'

His determination roused against him all the energies of samsara, the whole orientation of the mind towards selfishness and limiting views, which manifested in the form of the demonic figure of Mara. The demon rallied an army of hatred to break him, but the missiles hurled at him turned to flowers. Then Mara's daughters tried in vain to distract him with sensual thoughts. Finally Mara challenged him to produce a witness to his readiness for Enlightenment.

In reply Siddartha touched the earth, signalling a reconnection, both with the physical world that he had rejected and with his own body that he had denied. Then the earth shook and the earth goddess arose to confirm that Siddartha had through good deeds in many lifetimes earned his place on the Vajrasana - the mythical centre of the universe where all Buddhas become Enlightened. And Mara's army melted away.

In the first watch of the night Siddhartha recollected his previous lives, seeing the moral links between them, how the actions, habits and intentions of one life fed into the experience of the next. In the second watch he saw the same process in the lives of others. In the third watch he saw how the suffering in those lives was produced and how to be free from it.

He felt as if he had discovered an old and overgrown track leading to an ancient and sublime city. Who would he meet on that track?

MN 26. D 14. Mv. Lv

5. Compassion: Siddartha becomes the Buddha

As the dawn came up, his newly awakened mind no longer identified itself with the self-centred consciousness of Siddartha Gautama. He had become the Buddha, the Awakened One. He saw the way things are as a direct experience. Seeing how suffering and craving arose together, they both fell away from his mind. Nirvana, 'extinction' - of the driving forces of samsara - greed, hatred and delusion – had been attained.

He opened his eyes and saw the morning star. Then he affirmed to himself what had happened:

'In the endless round of living and dying,

I have long looked for the builder of this house.

Repeated birth is sorrowful.

Housebuilder, you are seen.

You shall not build the house again.

All your rafters are broken.

Your ridgepole is shattered.

My mind has gone to the unformed nirvana,

And reached the end of craving.'

For three weeks he absorbed his experience. Then storm clouds gathered, and as the first rain drops fell, the inner heat generated by his concentrated psychic energy manifested symbolically in the form of a serpent.

The serpent emerged from the roots of the tree where he sat and wrapped seven coils around him, spreading its hood above his head. After seven days the rain cleared and the serpent vanished, reappearing as a young man, Mucalinda the Serpent King, who bowed before returning to his kingdom under the earth. When he had gone the Buddha reflected,

'If the gods bow to me, where am I myself to worship?' And it occurred to him that he must worship the Dharma, the truth that had revealed itself to him.

He tried to engage a passing gentleman in conversation, but it did not come to anything. Afterwards the Buddha further reflected,

'This truth that I have realised is deep and subtle, beyond the logical tricks of the learned. It is useless to offer it to people who delight in sensual distractions and amassing wealth and reputation.'

At this thought, the chief of the gods, Brahmasahampati, appeared and begged him to teach,

'There are beings with only a little dust on their eyes', he said, 'who are losing their way through not hearing the Dharma.'

In a vision of compassion the Buddha surveyed the world and saw a lake full of lotuses. Some of them remained in the mud, others were reaching up through the water. But here and there lotus buds emerged above the water, and a few were opening to the sun. He said, 'Wide open are the doors of the Deathless.' The Buddha would teach the Dharma.

Dh 11. Vin. Mv 1. MN 26

6. The Four Noble Truths

The newly-Awakened Buddha was concerned to teach those 'with only a little dust in their eyes' first. He thought of communicating his realisation to his first teachers, but he became aware through his intuitive vision that they had recently died. Then he thought of his five friends who had abandoned him, and he knew where they would be.

A few days later his old friends, who were in the deer park at Varanasi, saw him in the distance, and they agreed not to defer to him as they used to. But when he came near they could not help getting him water and taking his robe and bowl. At once he let them know he was no longer simply the first amongst equals. 'I have attained freedom from death,' he said. They demurred, 'But you did not attain even when you were practising self-mortification. Now you have given up and reverted to luxury you must be even further from it.'

'Listen', he said. 'I have not given up or become self-indulgent just because I don't torment myself. On the contrary, I am fully Awakened. Have you ever heard me make such a claim before? Well then. I also know the path that leads to Awakening. It is neither the ordinary person's path of sensual pleasure, nor your path of self-mortification. Both these paths are self-centred, addictive and unaware.

I call the path I have found the *Middle Way*. It is based on a principle I call *conditionality*. Everything that exists is produced by conditions; when those conditions are removed, it ceases to exist. This applies to worlds, gods and ourselves. Nothing is eternal or has its own independent existence.

Above all, we can apply this principle to what gives us our experience of life: the mind and the suffering it makes for itself.

If we apply this principle to suffering, then, using the model of a medical diagnosis, we get what I call the four noble truths.

The first of these is suffering: life is always unsatisfactory in one way or another; even at its best, life always carries the seeds of loss and pain. This is the symptom.

The second is the origin of suffering, which is craving. This is the disease.

The third is how to bring an end to suffering. It is to bring an end to craving. This is the cure.

The fourth is the path to the cessation of suffering: the noble eightfold path. This is the treatment.'

Before going on to describe this treatment, the Buddha drew in the sand a wheel with eight spokes.

Vin. Mv 1. M26

7. The Noble Eightfold Path

What the Buddha proposed to his five old friends as the course of treatment for the suffering of life consisted in working on eight key aspects of human conditioning. The Buddhist path in this or any other form comprises the fourth noble truth.

'First, *Right View* is a conceptual understanding of the four noble truths. It is the view that evil action is that which is motivated by craving, hatred or delusion, and that it leads to suffering in this life and in future lives. It is the view that good action is that which is motivated by clear awareness and kindness, and that it leads to happiness.

Ultimately, however, right view is a freedom from views. Holding to nothing, eating just to live, the domain of the selfless is freedom, emptiness, the Unconditioned. Like the birds of the sky, they leave no tracks.

Right view does not cling to or insist on the existence or non-existence of either the self or the world. It avoids the wrong view of nihilism, the idea that at death you disappear; that your good or bad actions will not have an effect. It also avoids the wrong view of eternalism, the idea of a self or soul that exists as a separate unchanging entity and that reappears in future lives. At the same time it does not wriggle like an eel out of taking a clear position.

Secondly, *Right Intention* involves developing contentment and other positive emotions: kindness, compassion, feeling happy for others, and equanimity.

The next three steps are to do with ethics: *Right Speech* - truthful, kindly, harmonious, helpful, timely and courteous speech; *Right Action* - behaviour that is ethically aware; and *Right Livelihood*, which means gaining your living fairly and not trading in weapons, people, animals, alcohol or poison.

The final three steps are to do with meditation. The sixth is *Right Effort*. This is to sift out and keep out negative emotions, and to cultivate and maintain positive emotions. Finally there is *Right Mindfulness*, being deliberately attentive to one's experience, and *Right Concentration*, that is, focussing the mind in meditation.'

For several days they practised and talked, until finally the immaculate vision of the Dharma arose in one of the five friends, called Kondanya: 'All that is subject to arising is indeed subject to cessation.' The Buddha exclaimed, 'Kondanya knows! Kondanya knows!' The wheel of the Dharma had been turned.

After his success with these austere ascetics, the Buddha turned his attention to the urbane pleasure-seekers of the local city of Varanasi.

Dh Ch 7. DN 2. SN 12. MN 117

8. The story of the gilt slippers

At that time in the city of Varanasi there lived a young playboy called Yasa, son of a financial official. One morning he awoke early and looked around at his female companions, lying prostrate in sleep, like corpses. They were dishevelled, dribbling and snoring, and he was overcome with self-disgust. He slipped out of the house and made his way to the deer park, exclaiming 'It's all horrible!'

The Buddha was also there, walking, and as Yasa came near he spoke softly, inviting the youth out of his thoughts and into his immediate experience, 'Now, this is not horrible, here is nothing to fear. Sit. I will teach you.'

Suddenly hopeful, Yasa took off his gilt slippers, and sat down. The Buddha explained how happiness arises on the basis of ethics rather than indulgence, and then taught him the four noble truths. The young man's mind settled into a firm clarity of understanding which he proceeded to deepen in meditation.

Meanwhile his father had sent out search parties, and he himself went to look for his son in the deer park, where he eventually caught sight of the gilt slippers on the grass, and nearby the figure of the Buddha. 'Have you seen my son, Yasa?' he asked. Holding the old man's gaze the Buddha replied, 'Please sit. You will see Yasa before long.' He then engaged him in talk of generosity, of how giving liberates the mind from the distress of selfishness, and eventually Yasa's father became his first lay-disciple.

By this time, Yasa was fully liberated, his mind unencumbered by craving, hatred and delusion. Finally becoming aware of him there behind the Buddha, his father at once called him home, 'Yasa, your mother laments and grieves; come, restore her to life.'

But Yasa could not go back to his old life. 'Your son is now an arahant,' said the Buddha, 'how can you expect him to take an interest in the pursuit of sense pleasures?'

'I understand, Lord. This can only be for his happiness. But please come and eat at my house with Yasa as your attendant.'

Yasa requested ordination and the Buddha replied by way of acceptance, 'Ehi bikkhu (Come monk). Well taught is the Dharma. Lead a holy life for the utter extinction of suffering.'

Yasa's mother also became a lay-disciple. Four of his friends went to see for themselves why he had left their world of privilege behind, and ended up joining him as monks. Word got around, and before long there were fifty followers.

The Buddha soon became aware that some organisation would be needed.

Vn. Mv 1

9. An organisation of compassion

Speaking to his new disciples, the Buddha told them that he was simply the first among equals and that he had full confidence in them to teach the Dharma. They were all arahants, i.e. fully Enlightened individuals.

'Monks, I am free from the mind's fetters. You too are free from the mind's fetters. Go now and wander the roads for the benefit and happiness of others, out of compassion for the world. Teach the Dharma that is good in the beginning, good in the middle and good in the end. Teach the formulations of the Dharma that I have given you, but also communicate the meaning of it from your own experience.'

As more and more men were being received into the Order of monks, the Buddha realised that he needed to pass on some of his responsibilities. He said to them,

'I authorise you to confer the going forth into the homeless life and the admission into the Order wherever you happen to be. The prospective novice should prostrate at the feet of the monk ordaining him and kneeling with hands together he should say three times: 'I go for refuge to the Buddha, I go for refuge to the Dharma, I go for refuge to the Sangha.'' *

Soon after this the Buddha left Varanasi for Uruvela. On the way he was resting in a wood when a group of young men came by, distracted and out of breath. One of them said to him,

'Lord, have you seen a woman?'

'Boys,' he replied, 'what is your business with this woman?'

'We were enjoying a lunch party with our wives, but one of us had brought a prostitute with him, and she has disappeared with some of our jewellery.'

'I see, now just stop and think a moment. What is best, that you should seek a woman or that you should seek yourselves?'

'Lord, it is better to seek ourselves.'

'Then sit down and I will teach you the Dharma.'

So he did, and one by one, as the afternoon faded into evening, they all awakened to a clear vision of the truth and were admitted to the Order of monks.

The Buddha's teaching continued to be welcomed by wandering seekers after truth and the wealthy young men of the cities. But next he sought a very different encounter – with the ancient Brahminical tradition of fire worship and animal sacrifice.

Vin. Mv 1

This statement, the Threefold Refuge, also known as Going for Refuge to the 3 Jewels, is the statement of faith repeated by all Buddhists up to the present day.

10. Delusion: the matted haired fire-worshippers

The Buddha generally poured scorn on the display of paranormal feats to impress ordinary people. However, he always spoke to people in their own language, exploring their own values in their own terms, and in the following encounter, the language they understood was one of miracles and wonder-working.

Arriving at Uruvela from Varanasi the Buddha sought out Kassapa of Uruvela, one of three brothers, each the teacher of many hundreds of fire-worshipping matted-haired ascetics, and asked to spend the night in his worship-room. Kassapa consented, but warned, 'Beware the venomous serpent of supernormal powers that dwells there lest it take your life.' Unmoved, the Buddha entered the room, saw that he had provoked the snake, which was spitting fire, and sat down mindfully. He focussed his energies into the element of fire, till flames leapt from his own body, and the room glowed hot in the darkness. At dawn he emerged with the serpent curled up placidly in his bowl.

As he welcomed him, Kassapa reflected to himself, 'The monk has great powers, but he is no arahant as I am.'

During the following nights the forest where the Buddha was residing was lit up by what seemed to be pillars of fire, but were in fact various divinities who came to hear his teaching. Again Kassapa was impressed, but he reassured himself, 'he is no arahant as I am'.

However, as the day of a big public sacrificial ceremony was approaching Kassapa secretly feared that his guest's presence would upstage him. Knowing his fears, the Buddha chose not to attend. When Kassapa discovered that the Buddha had read his mind, he still comforted himself with the thought, 'But after all he is no arahant as I am'.

That year the rains came early and the river flooded. Kassapa took a boat to rescue the Buddha, but found him walking dry-foot amidst the flood. The Buddha leapt across the surging waters and landed softly in the boat; but looking at Kassapa, he saw that Kassapa still clung to his view of himself as an arahant, and so he decided it was time to put him right: 'Kassapa you are not near to being an arahant'. At this Kassapa prostrated himself at the feet of the Buddha.

In due course Kassapa's many disciples, having watched the whole drama unfold, were happy to follow his lead. Later, when his brothers saw discarded matted locks and the paraphernalia of the fire worship drifting past them down the river they went to investigate, and they too, with their disciples, were accepted into the Sangha.

Vin: Mv 1

11. Attachment: the Fire Sermon

Having converted the Kassapa brothers and their fire-worshipping followers, the Buddha addressed them, near Gaya, with the celebrated 'fire sermon'.

'All the world is on fire: the senses are burning; sense objects and contact with them burn; consciousness burns; feelings, whether pleasant or painful, burn; the mind and its objects burn. Life burns. It burns with the fire of craving, hatred and delusion; with birth, ageing and death; with sorrow and pain. Seeing this, the wise person does not lose their awareness in the senses or their objects, or in thoughts, or in feelings of pleasure or pain. In this way one becomes dispassionate, craving and hatred fade away, and the heart is liberated.'

From Gaya the Buddha led his Sangha to Rajagaha, capital of the Kingdom of Magadha. There King Bimbisara went to meet him, accompanied by hundreds of dignitaries. None could believe that Kassapa the Great had submitted himself to another teacher.

So the Buddha nudged Kassapa, 'Tell them why you left off asceticism, sacrifice and fire-worship.'

He replied, 'I saw that the reward I sought was always personal advantage; it was just a spiritual extension of mundane vanities. Then I took no more joy in it.'

'Where is your joy now then?'

'I saw a state of peace, where nothing is owned, where one is not possessed by the senses, where there is no otherness, no being led by others.' And then he prostrated himself before the Buddha.

That day King Bimbisara became a lay disciple, and he presented the Sangha with the Bamboo Grove near Rajagaha. Bimbisara's sister Mallika, who was Queen to King Pasenadi of Kosala, the other great regional power, also became a disciple.

Three years later, the Buddha was in the capital of Kosala, Savatthi, when a citizen came to see him because his son had died: 'Help me' he said, 'I am beside myself with grief'. The Buddha responded simply, 'Those who are dear to us bring us sorrow.'

The citizen was disgusted with this reply, as were others he spoke to. 'Dear ones' they affirmed, 'are a comfort and a joy'. King Pasenadi agreed when he heard the story, and mocked Mallika for believing everything her precious teacher said. So she explained how all things change, how our attachments naturally resist this truth, and how sorrow follows upon that resistance. Struck by the realisation that insecurity and loss shadowed all that he relished, Pasenadi eventually became a disciple as well.

Attachment is not just to people and things. At the deepest level, the Buddha's teaching addressed attachment to views.

Vin. Mv 1. S 35. M 87

12. The Buddha confronts Nihilism

Sariputta and Moggallana were childhood friends from near Rajagaha. One day they were watching a tale being enacted by travelling entertainers and when they emerged from the enchantment of the story they realised that their whole life was like this, a make-believe dream. So they left home and became disciples of Sanjaya, the great sceptic and nihilist teacher of that time.

It was the winter after the Buddha's Enlightenment when Sariputta caught sight of a monk gathering alms, whose mindful deportment impressed him vividly. The monk was Assaji, one of the first five disciples of the Buddha. Sariputta asked him who his teacher was and what he taught. Assaji said, 'I am a beginner; all I know is this:

'The Tathagatha has explained the origin of those things that proceed from a cause. Their cessation too he has explained.'

Sariputta understood that the title Tathagatha, used here in place of Buddha, carried two opposite meanings: 'thus come' and 'thus gone'. It meant one who has gone from the world of suffering and who has come back, out of compassion. He also intuited the Buddha's primary insight – that mind-made suffering is the product of conditions and that those conditions may be reversed.

Sariputta lost no time in passing his discovery on to Moggallana. They then explained to Sanjaya why they were leaving the group and persuaded his other 250 followers to go with them.

The two friends would become the Buddha's chief disciples, but throughout his illustrious life Sariputta would revere the humble Assaji whom he always regarded as his teacher.

Sariputta became fully Enlightened after he overheard the Buddha talking to a wanderer called Dighanakka who denied the validity of any religious position whatsoever. Everything, he held, is relative; therefore no ethical judgement can have any meaning.

The Buddha said that holding to no view was itself a view. He pointed out that you cannot help holding views, that your deepest views are unconscious assumptions about how things are. The goal for his followers was to be free of *attachment* to views, to stop creating delusion, hatred and craving out of them, and this meant taking up clear views that would lead to this goal.

'If you hold a religious view and identify with it, saying, 'This alone is true; all else is false', you become dogmatic and disputatious. The same goes for rejecting such views – you still become dogmatic and disputatious. Myself, I am not a dogmatist but an analyst. When you experience how things really are, then all attachment to fixed views or anything else fades away.'

Vin. Mv 1. MN 74

13. Nanda and the path of bliss

A year after his Enlightenment, and seven years after his disappearance, the Buddha returned home to Kapilavastu, and went begging through the town where he used to be an aristocrat.

At first his father resented this affront to the family honour, but the Buddha explained that he now belonged to a more ancient and noble lineage, whose honour lay in holding out a bowl for alms. Eventually his father became a lay-disciple, as did his wife and his aunt. A number of cousins also joined the Order.

One day, the Buddha was guest of honour at a feast for his half-brother Nanda, who was about to be married and consecrated as the new family heir. When the Buddha left, he handed his bowl to Nanda to carry for him. With one backward look at his wife, Nanda followed his half-brother out of the bright, cheerful hall into the darkness of the forest.

Arriving at the monks' encampment the Buddha turned to Nanda and asked if he wanted to be ordained. In awe of his half-brother, Nanda said 'Yes'. However, Nanda did not take to the life easily. He remained a hedonist, and the Buddha had to remind him that it did not befit a monk to wear eye make-up, iron his robe and get himself a nice glazed bowl.

Eventually Nanda decided to give up and go home to his wife. He said to the Buddha, 'I just can't forget her face when I looked back at her for the last time, the way she held her hair back as she said, 'Come back soon, Prince'.

The Buddha persuaded him to persist with his practice by showing him a vision of dove-footed nymphs in a heaven realm, available to those proficient in meditation. Nanda began to enjoy the bliss of the stabilised mind by concentrating on this goal but the other monks ridiculed him for practising the Dharma for the sake of the dove-footed nymphs. 'You've sold yourself,' they said. Ashamed, he applied himself to reflection on the impermanent and insubstantial nature of the heaven realms, until he attained Enlightenment.

During the Buddha's time in Kapilavastu his wife sent his young son Rahula to ask him for his inheritance, meaning to remind the Buddha of his worldly responsibilities. Rahula went up to his father and said, 'Your shadow is pleasant, monk'. Then he asked for his inheritance and the Buddha ordained him there and then.

As his son grew up the Buddha gave him a great deal of tender attention.

SN 21.8. Dh com 1.13, 14. Vin. Mv. Kh. 1.54. Lv

14. Reflection: the Buddha teaches his son

One evening when the boy was eleven, the Buddha went to visit his son, and as he washed he scooped a few drops of water into the water-dipper and said, 'Look, Rahula, people who tell lies have as little good in them as this.' Then he threw the drops away and said, 'See, if people tell lies, the good in them is thrown away like that.' Then, turning the dipper upside-down, he said, 'The monk who tells lies, his whole life is made worthless like that,' and, as he turned it back he said 'And it becomes as empty of good as that.'

'Think of a king's elephant, Rahula, with huge tusks, strong, brave and intelligent. In battle he may skilfully use each of his feet, and his tusks, but if he keeps his trunk back, he will be kept back for more training. He is not ready. So don't tell a lie, even for a joke.'

'What is a mirror for, Rahula?' 'It is to reflect.' 'Whatever you do, say or even think, hold a mirror to it in your mind, so that you see its nature clearly. Then reflect - will it be harmful? If so, abandon it and confess it. If it is helpful, then cultivate it.'

Some years later, when the two of them were walking into Savatthi for alms, the Buddha became aware that his son was thinking about what his life would have been like had his father become a king. So the Buddha taught him to reflect more deeply, especially in his meditation.

'Reflect on the five elements: first earth – the solidity of things; then water - all that is fluid; next fire - temperature; fourthly air – all that is gaseous; and finally space - the sense of extension in all directions. Reflect on each one separately, both as it features in the external world, and within the body. Then reflect with regard to each of these elements - This is not mine; I am not this; this is not myself. By regarding the body as an impermanent collection of processes that must return to where they came from you will gradually relinquish your identification with the body as a permanent entity.'

The Buddha also taught Rahula to reflect on his identification with his passing mental states. 'Be like the earth, Rahula,' he said, 'it deals with what is clean and dirty, pleasant and unpleasant, just the same. It doesn't get excited or angry or disgusted. Be like earth, water, fire, air and space with regard to whatever comes before your attention.'

M. 61, 62, 147

15. Giving: the world's first monastery

For the first three years the Buddha's monks, or *bikkhus*, always lived out in the open, even during the rainy season.

Then a rich merchant had some huts built for them in the Bamboo Grove near Rajagaha. On completion he invited the whole Sangha for a meal, and his brother-in-law Anathapindika, who had arrived in town that day, was surprised to find him too busy to welcome him. He thought he must have invited King Bimbisara himself.

'No, I'm inviting the Buddha and his Sangha.'
'The Buddha?' said Anathapindika.
'That's right'.
'Did you say the Buddha?'
'Yes.'
'You mean it's possible to find a fully Enlightened one here today?'
'Well, tomorrow at least'.

In excited anticipation, Anathapindika got up three times during the night, thinking it must already be morning. Finally he hurried nervously out of the city gates, and as the light came up he saw someone walking up and down who beckoned him over. Anathapindika prostrated before him and asked him if he had slept well. The Buddha said that having forsaken all attachments he suffered no inner conflict and slept in bliss. After some talk of the path of ethics Anathapindika left joyfully, and the next day he gave a meal to the Sangha, at which he invited the Buddha and his monks to spend the rains in retreat at his own city of Savatthi.

When Anathapindika returned home he looked round Savatthi for a park to give to the monks. Eventually he came to the pleasure park of Prince Jeta, and offered to buy it. Prince Jeta shook his head: 'I'm not selling – unless you want to spread a hundred thousand gold coins over it.' 'I'll take it then' responded Anathapindika. 'But it's not for sale.' said Prince Jeta. Anathapindika was determined and went to the lawyers who said, 'If you set a value on the park, and someone comes up with the price, it's sold.' So he had carts of gold brought up and spread them over the park, till there was just a corner left uncovered, and Prince Jeta said, 'Let that be my gift'. Then Anathapindika had huts and halls built in the park, with drying rooms, store houses, latrines, ponds, well rooms and bathrooms.

Many years later, when Anathapindika was dying, Sariputta instructed him in meditation and in the analytical mind-training practices that were reserved for the monks. Inspired by this teaching Anathapindika wept. He said that such teachings should be more available to the laity, as some of them had only a little dust on their eyes.

Vin. Cv 6. S 10. M 143

16. The admission of women into the Order

It was the sixth year of the Buddha's ministry, the Buddha's father had died, and the Buddha had returned to his native city of Kapilavastu to broker a peace between the Shakyans and the Koliyans who were in dispute over irrigation rights from the river that divided them.

Being newly widowed, the Buddha's foster mother, Mahapajapati Gotami, came to him to ask that women might be accepted into the Sangha; the Buddha refused. Shortly afterwards he set out for Vaisali. Meanwhile Mahapajapati, along with some other Sakyan women, cut off her hair and donned yellow robes and made her own way to Vaisali. There she stood with the other women outside the Gabled Hall in the Great Wood where the Buddha was staying. Her feet were swollen, and the dust on her face was channelled by tears.

The Buddha's attendant, Ananda, asked her what the matter was. She told him of the Buddha's rejection of her request. So he asked the Buddha to reconsider, 'Are women capable of becoming Enlightened?' 'Yes of course,' said the Buddha. 'Then' Ananda went on, 'considering that Mahapajapati was a good foster mother to you after your own mother died...'

The Buddha gave way but on condition that nuns accept eight extra rules which, amongst other things, made the most senior nuns pay homage to the most junior monk, and disallowed nuns from giving teachings to monks. She accepted them gladly, as if they were 'a garland of lotuses'. Afterwards the Buddha predicted that with the formation of the order of nuns his teaching would survive only 500 years, half as long as it would have done otherwise.

Well-known as it is, this story is probably unreliable. Ananda was not in fact the Buddha's attendant at this time. Nor is it likely that the Buddha could have been cajoled into a decision of this magnitude, and with such dire and apparently foreseeable consequences. It may be that the compilers of the records had little enthusiasm for the order of nuns, and made the famously well-meaning Ananda responsible for the decision by introducing him into the episode. In the end, of the Buddha's 80 foremost disciples 12 were women, including Dhammadinna, 'foremost in giving teachings'.

The Buddha insisted that Enlightenment was no respecter of status. It was available to everyone, monk, nun, novice, or lay person. Individuals of a dominant caste or gender had no more special status for him than the gods themselves.

'The gods envy those who control their senses as a charioteer controls his horses. Better than winning a thousand battles is to conquer yourself. No god or demon can overturn that victory.'

Vin. Cv 10. A. 8. Dh 7, 8

17. Friendship: the Buddha's attendants

Ananda was just the last of a series of personal attendants who controlled the flow of visitors to the Buddha and provided him with companionship. Originally, monks had taken it in turns to fulfil this role, with mixed results. One of them, Sunnakkhatta, left the Sangha altogether, being last heard of going about Vaisali denigrating the Buddha's teaching.

In the 13th year of his mission the Buddha had an attendant called Meghiya. One day Meghiya was returning from his alms round in the village of Jantu when he caught sight of a delightful mango grove on the banks of the river Kimikala. He thought this would be the perfect place to meditate and finally become Enlightened, and he hurried back to the Buddha and breathlessly told him of his plan. 'So would you mind, Lord,' he concluded, 'if I went off for the afternoon?'

The Buddha said, 'As I am on my own, I'd be grateful if you'd stay until another monk arrives.' Meghiya felt frustrated, 'It is all very well for you, Lord, you are already Enlightened. But I am not; I still have my work to complete.'

The Buddha tried to dissuade him, but he had no command over his disciples. 'As you talk of work, Meghiya, what can I say? Do as you think fit.' So Meghiya spent the afternoon meditating and came back to report that his mind had been overwhelmed by hindrances, with sexual fantasies and resentful thoughts.

The Buddha replied, 'When the heart is not yet fully liberated, you need five things.

First, make a delightful friendship with those who support your practice. Second, train yourself in morality; be conscious of the smallest faults and the danger in them. Third, take care over your speech; what you talk about will deeply affect your states of mind. Fourth, eliminate negative mental states and develop positive ones. And fifth, notice, reflect on and take in the coming into being and passing of things till insight arises.'

After twenty years the Buddha took on his cousin Ananda as a permanent attendant. Ananda was loyal, friendly and personable; he also committed all the Buddha's teachings to his phenomenal memory. Hence they all begin with the words, 'Thus have I heard,' meaning this is how Ananda heard it.

One day, Ananda remarked to the Buddha, 'It seems to me, Lord, that friendship is half of the spiritual life'. The Buddha replied, 'Not at all, Ananda, friendship is the whole of the spiritual life.'

The Buddha made healthy relationships the key to ordinary life as well as to the life of a monk.

Ud 4.1

18. The Buddha's guide to ordinary happiness

The Buddha was concerned that people should be happy and successful. If they aimed to attain the happiness and success of Enlightenment, then they needed to follow the complete noble eightfold path. In doing so they might then find themselves held back by the attachment that tended to come with possessions. But poverty was not a value in itself. For lay people, being rich enabled them to benefit many more people. As the Buddha suggests in the following teaching, success for a lay-person depended on their being ethical and looking after their relationships.

A boy from Rajagaha called Sigalaka was mourning his father, and to fulfil the old man's dying wish he went every morning to the Bamboo Grove to perform an ancient ritual of making full prostrations to the six directions. One day the Buddha approached him and advised him of a better way to respect his father's memory:

'First, be aware of your ethics. Avoid taking life, stealing, sexual misconduct, and telling lies. Then examine the motivation for your actions; avoid acting out of craving, hatred, fear, or thoughtlessness. Next look at how you make use of your energy - don't waste your resources through drink or drugs, roaming the streets at all hours, frequenting places of trivial amusement, gambling, or making endless excuses not to get down to work.

The Buddha went on to talk about friendships. 'Avoid' he said, 'those who are full of goodwill, but never able to help at a critical time owing to a problem of their own, and who praise you to your face whilst criticising you behind your back. Steer clear of gamblers, cheats, addicts or bullies, and those who encourage and indulge your weaknesses.

'On the other hand stick to those friends who will look out for you when you cannot do so yourself (for example when intoxicated), who will share their secrets with you and keep yours, who will take genuine pleasure in your good fortune, and who will give their life for you if need be.'

'If you want to salute the six directions,' the Buddha went on, 'give them some real meaning. For example, make each of them represent a particular kind of relationship in your life. So make the east symbolise the relationship of parent and child; the south, teacher and student; the west, husband and wife; the north, friends; the earth below, employer and employee; and the sky above, monks and lay-people. Each of these relationships brings with it a specific set of duties. You worship the six directions by honouring those responsibilities to others.'

DN 31. AN 3

19. Patience. The story of Sundari

The Buddha's Sangha depended on lay-people like Sigalaka for food and support. However, it was just one of many sects of wanderers in northern India. A degree of jealousy arose from the fact that the Buddhists were better respected and honoured than others and, as a result, were better fed and given pleasant parks in which to spend the rainy season.

It was while the Buddha was staying at the Jeta Grove near Savatthi that certain wanderers who had become jealous of his pre-eminence approached a female cousin of theirs called Sundari, who was also a wanderer, and asked her to visit the Jeta Grove on a regular basis. When they knew that she had been seen by enough people visiting the Buddhist retreat site they murdered her and buried her in a ditch there.

Then they went to King Pasanedi of Kosala and obtained his authorisation to make a search of the Jeta Grove for their cousin. Finding her where they had buried her they carried her through the streets, reviling the Buddhists for the despicable act of taking their pleasure from a woman and then killing her. 'Call yourselves monks?' they cried. They encouraged the people of Savatthi to join them in hurling abuse at the Buddhists: 'Heartless lechers! Shame on you bunch of hypocrites.'

The Buddha told the monks not to react to these slanders, and within a week the outcry had died down.

The Buddha's teaching in relation to this situation was that his followers always had something far more valuable to guard than what their anger might defend.

He was once being abused by a Brahmin who wanted to test the Buddha's equanimity. The Buddha asked him, 'If you were to offer someone a gift and they refused it, to whom would it belong?' 'To me of course', the Brahmin replied. 'The same goes for your abuse', the Buddha concluded gently, 'It is yours to deal with.'

On another occasion the Buddha said to his followers:

'I shall patiently endure abuse, just as the trained elephant endures the arrows of battle. Other people cannot be expected to be considerate.

It is an old saying: 'they'll blame you if you are silent; they'll blame you if you talk a lot; they'll blame you if you say little. No-one escapes blame in this world. Curb your anger in your body. Curb it in your speech. Curb it in your mind.'

Speak gently, and let your mind be quiet like a broken gong. A mind without anger is free.'

Ud 4. 8. Dh 17, 23

20. Abandoning violence: 'Finger-necklace', the serial killer

In the twentieth year of his teaching the Buddha came to hear that a forested road out of Savatthi was being terrorised by a serial killer. The murderer wore the fingers of his victims in a necklace, and so was called Angulimala, or 'Finger-necklace'.

One day the Buddha set out on that road alone, ignoring repeated warnings from local farmers that Angulimala would even pick off people who travelled in large groups, one by one.

Catching sight of the Buddha entering the forest Angulimala took up his weapons and hurried down to the road. But when he set off in pursuit he found that even though the figure ahead walked at a slow steady pace he could not catch him, however fast he ran. Baffled, he halted, shouting 'Stop, monk!'

The Buddha replied, 'I have stopped. Now you too must stop.'

Angulimala was quite thrown by the fearless monk and his riddles. 'What do you mean? It is I who have stopped. You are walking still.'

The Buddha explained: 'I have abandoned harming any living being. This is my stopping. I have come to the end of myself. But your violence is headlong, without restraint.'

Angulimala threw down his weapons and fell at the Buddha's feet. 'Come, bikkhu', said the Buddha, and Angulimala went with him as his new disciple to Savatthi. There, the king himself gave the killer-turned-monk the protection due to a member of the Buddha's Sangha, such was the respect in which the Buddha was held.

One morning on his alms round Angulimala saw a woman enduring an intensely painful labour with a deformed child. He felt overwhelmed by the suffering that people go through and he later expressed his feelings to the Buddha, who told him,

'Go back to that woman and say, 'Sister, since I was born I have never taken life. By that truth may you and the child have peace.'' The truth was that with the arising of compassion Angulimala had been reborn and had harmed no-one since then. And when he repeated the Buddha's words to the woman she and her child were restored to well-being.

Some time after Angulimala gained Enlightenment he was recognised as 'finger-necklace' and beaten up in the town. When he returned to the Jeta Grove, with his head gashed and his robes torn, the Buddha said to him, 'Bear this willingly for the sake of the suffering in many future lives that you have avoided through your Awakening in this life.' In his meditation Angulimala longed for those who hated him to taste the bliss of the Dharma.

MN 86

21. Shame and ethics

Ugga was a wealthy banker of the city of Hatthigama. He had been feasting and drinking heavily over several days, and had gone for some fresh air to the park outside the city with his friends and some girls, when he almost fell over the figure of the Buddha sitting mindfully under a tree. The others went on their way merrily, but as he stopped before the Buddha, shame swept through Ugga like a tide - and his intoxication vanished.

For the Buddha shame was a powerfully positive emotion, and he took advantage of it to explain to Ugga the direct, natural link between ethical behaviour and happiness, both in this life and future lives. He distinguished between conventional morality, which varies between one culture and another, and natural morality, which has a direct positive effect on the human mind, whatever one's background. Ugga was deeply receptive to what he was saying, and before they had finished talking he had not only changed his life, but his vision of the truth had become unobstructed.

The Buddha offered him five moral precepts or training principles to undertake: to abstain from harming living beings, stealing, sexual misconduct, false speech, and intoxication.

These five precepts are followed by all Buddhists. They were training principles because the Buddha identified morality as a skill to be developed, not a set of commandments.

On another occasion the Buddha was speaking to a silversmith called Cunda about purifying rituals. He said that true purification lay in ten 'paths of skilful action', replacing the fifth of the five precepts (the body precepts) with three more speech precepts and three mind precepts. The extra precepts were to abstain from harsh speech, frivolous speech, slanderous speech, covetousness, hatred and wrong views.

Because the Buddha's ethics was about training, he emphasised moral habits:

'Be quick to do the right thing. Delay, and a morally unskilful impulse will take over.

Do not underestimate evil, thinking, 'Just this once won't do any harm'. A jug fills drop by drop, and the fool fills himself with evil bit by bit.

Do not underestimate good, thinking, 'It's not worth bothering – it won't do any good'. You become full to the brim with good, drop by drop.'

As well as strictly ethical precepts, the monks were given over 200 rules of monastic discipline – for example, not being alone with someone of the opposite sex, not handling money, and not eating after midday. Breaches of ethics and discipline were regularly confessed.

AN 4, 5. MN 114. DN 5. Dh 9

22. Confession and the ocean of the Dharma

The Sangha observed the unwritten ethical code of the wandering holy men, which ensured the respect of the laity on whom they depended for alms: no killing, no sex, no stealing, no false claims to spiritual attainments. As well as this, on full moon and new moon days they met together and after confessing any ethical failures they recited the Pratimoksha:

'Avoid wrongdoing. Act skilfully. Purify the heart. This is the Buddha's teaching.

'Patient forbearance is the ultimate practice. Freedom from craving and hatred is the ultimate goal. This is the testimony of the Awakened Ones. No-one who harms or persecutes anyone is a real member of the Sangha.

'Do not hurt or find fault. Observe the rules of the Order. Be moderate in diet. Seek seclusion. Meditate intently. This is the Buddha's message.'

One night in Savatthi, the monks sat waiting for the Buddha to begin reciting the Pratimoksha. They waited and waited. Dawn was breaking when finally the Buddha announced, 'The assembly is not pure'. Moggallana looked around and with his fabled power of reading minds he saw that one of the monks was 'a fraud, corrupt and secretive in his habits.' He took the monk by the arm and led him out. From this point the Buddha left responsibility for the Order's harmony to the Order itself. He said,

'Things rot when you keep them wrapped up. Uncover what is concealed, lest it rot.'

He went on to compare the Dharma to the Ocean:

> 'As the ocean shelves down, so development in the Dharma is piecemeal, without an unprepared penetration of final knowledge.
>
> As the ocean keeps within the bounds of the land, so the Sangha is bound by its rules.
>
> As the ocean casts ashore a dead body, so the Sangha casts out one who is a fraud, corrupt and secretive.
>
> As the great rivers give up their status when they join the sea, so individuals within the Sangha surrender their caste.
>
> As the sea can take any amount of water flowing into it, so there is no limit to the possible numbers of those who Awake.
>
> As the ocean has one taste, the taste of salt, so the Dharma has one taste, the taste of freedom.
>
> As the ocean holds many treasures, so is the Dharma full of precious teachings.
>
> As the ocean contains monsters of the deep, so is the Dharma the abode of formidable individuals.'

As well as comparing the Dharma to the ocean, at other times the Buddha compared it to a raft – and even a snake.

Vin Cv 9. Ud 5.5

23. Understanding the Dharma: 3 parables

At one time there was a monk called Arittha, formerly a vulture trainer, who went about saying that there was no harm in indulging in negative emotions. The Buddha called for him:

'Arittha, it is easy to get a wrong idea of the Dharma. If you take it up in order to be holier-than-thou or to have something impressive to say you are going down a dangerous path. It is like picking up a water snake. If you grasp the snake by its tail, it is likely to bite you; but if you pin it with a cleft stick you can pick it up safely. Likewise with the Dharma. Beware of learning the words without putting them to their proper use.

The Buddha often compared the Dharma with a raft, warning his followers not to lose sight of the fact that it has a purpose beyond itself.

'If you build a raft to cross over a river, you won't think, having crossed safely over, 'What a useful raft; I must carry it with me.' You will leave it behind. So it is with the Dharma. When you reach the further shore, when you attain nirvana, it is to be left behind.'

On another occasion a monk called Malunkyaputta said to the Buddha, 'You seem to evade certain important questions. Are body and consciousness the same stuff or are they separate? Is the universe eternal? Is it infinite? And what happens to the Enlightened mind after death? If you do not know the answers it would be more honest to frankly admit it. Then I can just return to the lay life.'

'Malunkyaputta,' said the Buddha, 'did I ever say to you, 'Come, be my disciple and I will tell you if the world is eternal or not?' 'No Lord' he replied. 'And did you say to me 'Satisfy me on these points and I will be your disciple'. 'No Lord,' he admitted again. The Buddha concluded, 'You are like a man who has been shot by an arrow, and with a doctor ready to treat him he says, 'Wait, don't get that arrow out until I know who shot the arrow, with what kind of bow, using what kind of bowstring and what the arrow was made of. You would be dead before you found out. I teach that there is suffering, the origin of suffering, the cessation of suffering and the way leading to the cessation of suffering.'

On another occasion the Buddha explained how, without this clarity, religious beliefs lend their ideals to anger and violence.

M 22, 64

24. Religious disputes: the blind men and the elephant

One day various wanderers of differing views ran into one another in Savatthi and began squabbling and brawling. Some were vehement that the world is eternal, others that it is impermanent. Some insisted that the world must be finite, others asserted the opposite view with equal force. Some proclaimed the folly of holding to the view that the body and soul are identical; others lambasted the idea that they could be distinct. 'Here is the truth of things!' 'No, you are wrong, this is the how things are!' When this was reported to the Buddha in the Jeta Grove, he told this story:

'There was once a king of this city who ordered all the blind men of the city to be gathered together. An elephant was brought forward and the blind men were each placed where they could reach out and feel with their hands one part of it. They were then asked to describe what an elephant was like.

'A water pot,' said the man on its head. 'A winnowing basket,' said the man placed by the ear. 'No, a ploughshare' said the man holding a tusk. 'You're wrong, it's like a plough-pole' said the man feeling the trunk. 'Not at all, it's like a granary' said the man with his arms outstretched across the belly. 'Pillars,' said the man holding the legs. 'On the contrary, it's a kind of bowl for pounding' said the man on its back. 'Totally off the mark. It's a pounding implement,' said the man underneath the elephant. The man grasping the tail shook his head: 'A kind of broom', he said firmly. Before long the blind men had come to blows over their views.

'In this way,' the Buddha concluded, 'people identify themselves with a limited view or interpretation of the truth and lose their way.'

The Buddha's aunt Mahapajapati once asked the Buddha how to tell the Dharma from false teachings. He said, 'Be guided by a clear awareness of your own mental states: whatever leads to serenity, to being unfettered, to letting go, to modesty, to contentment, to integration and concentration, to energy in pursuit of the good - that is the Dharma.'

Questioned as to why people fall into doctrinal disputing, the Buddha said it was out of attachment to preferences, and out of thinking oneself superior, inferior or equal to others. 'Someone who knows the truth does not dispute it.'

A view that the Buddha saw as unhelpful in this respect was the belief in a creator God.

Udana 6.4. Vin Cv 10. A 8. SN 4. Dh 10

25. Miracles: The Buddha and God

The gods are at a disadvantage in terms of developing wisdom because their primary experience is of bliss, with little sense of the first noble truth of suffering. They do not feel their own impermanence. This includes great Brahma himself, who is under the impression that he created the universe simply because he was there at the beginning. The Buddha explored this issue in discussion with a lay follower, Kevaddha, in the city of Nalanda.

Kevaddha suggested that if the Buddha performed miracles he would deepen the faith of his followers. The Buddha responded:

'There are three kinds of miracle: firstly, psychic powers such as levitation, walking on water and visiting the heavens; secondly, mind-reading; thirdly, teaching the Dharma. The first two can always be explained away by sceptics. The third is the one that matters. Why this is so I shall explain with a story'.

'There was a monk who wrestled with a difficult question: where does the universe consisting in the four material elements come to an end? As he had developed the power of visiting the heaven realms he decided to get his answer from those he thought would be best placed to know.

'The gods of the first realm he visited pleaded ignorance and passed him on to the realm of the thirty-three gods. But nor could they help, so he tried the gods of the Tusita heaven, who referred him to a yet higher plane. So it went on. Finally, he found himself amongst the heavenly host praising Great Brahma himself. He asked where Brahma was and they said that when a certain radiance shone forth, he would appear. And so it proved. So the monk put his question to Brahma, who replied, 'Monk, I am the all-seeing, all-powerful, Lord and creator of all, Father of all that has been and shall be.' 'Excellent,' said the monk, 'then I'm sure you can answer my question.' As it became clear that the monk would not be put off, Brahma took him aside.

'Look Monk, these hosts of angelic beings believe I am omniscient, so this is just for your ears: I have no idea. Go and ask the Buddha.' So he did.

'I answered that earth, water, fire and air do not come to an end apart from the sense-based dualistic consciousness they depend upon in order to be perceived and distinguished. They dissolve where consciousness is undefined by its objects, boundless and luminous.'

Not being a god, the Buddha laid down no commandments. With the idea of karma he did not need to.

DN 11

26. Karma

The Buddha adapted the idea of karma from the Indian culture of his time. Karma means 'action' in the sense of having consequences. Originally it was a primitive belief that certain ritual actions, especially sacrifice, would produce certain physical results. This belief was re-interpreted by Nathaputta, the founder of Jainism, in terms of ethics. It was understood that a morally good action would constitute positive karma and produce a positive result for the person concerned. So the law of karma offered a natural connection between ethics and one's experience of life; it was a moral feedback system. Ethical behaviour was a matter of skill rather than obedience. The Buddha interpreted it even more radically.

Whereas the Jains believed that karma meant primarily physical action, the Buddha's position was that karma was primarily about intention.

He was once visited in Nalanda by a Jain layman called Upali who had promised his teacher that 'just as a strong man seizing a long-haired ram by its fleece, might drag it along', so he would convert the Buddha to the Jain position. In the event, the Buddha persuaded Upali that it was your conscious choice of action that determined the ethical weight of an action. And he encouraged his new convert to continue to give alms to the Jains who were dependent on his support.

In another meeting with some Jains, the Buddha refuted their idea that you can burn off negative karma by self-inflicted suffering. He also firmly resisted the idea of karma as the cast-iron reason for everything. If you suffer, he maintained, it is unlikely to be the karmic result of something you did in a previous life.

'Otherwise, with this view, you get people who become murderers, thieves, fornicators and liars on account of their karma, their previous unskilful action.' Any moral responsibility for their actions, any free-will, any possibility to change, he said, then becomes impossible. Karma, he said, is just one amongst a number of conditions, including biological and environmental factors, that gives people their experience.

In this way the Buddha made karma less about cosmic justice, and more about the development of a positive character through positive choices of action. To a young man who asked him why life was so unfair, the Buddha said, 'You are the heir to your actions. They make you who you are.'

The Buddha took an even more radical view of rebirth. He introduced the idea of karma working at a moment-by-moment level: at every moment the individual is in a sense 'reborn' as a result of their previous actions.

MN 56, 101. SN 36. AN iii

27. What is reborn?

One day in the Jeta Grove a wanderer called Vacchagotta came and asked the Buddha, 'Does the self exist?' The Buddha stayed silent. 'So,' said the visitor, 'does it not exist?' The Buddha said nothing. After a while the man got up and left, and Ananda asked the Buddha why he hadn't answered. The Buddha said, 'It is true that the self does not exist. But Vacchagotta is not ready to hear that. He would have gone away with the sense that the self he used to have has been taken from him.'

On another occasion a nun called Vajira provided the Buddha with an image for what he meant. 'Just as we give the term 'chariot' to various bits of wood and metal and leather that are put together in a certain way, so we give the term 'self' to a different set of elements: form, feeling, perception, intention, consciousness.' Both are real, but only as a complex of conditions.

In particular, the self is real as a sense of moral responsibility.

One day while he was on his alms round the Buddha was approached by a naked ascetic called Kassapa who insisted on asking him a question: 'Is my suffering created, speaking in terms of karma, by myself?'

'No' the Buddha replied. A further series of questions followed: 'Is it created by another?' 'No'. 'Is it created by both myself and another?' 'No'. 'So is there no connection between unskilful action and suffering?' 'No.' 'Are you saying then that there is no suffering?'

'No,' said the Buddha. 'I teach the Middle Way. To say that the person who experiences the karmic result of an action is the same as the person who performs the action is eternalism, a wrong view. But to say they are different is nihilism, also a wrong view.'

The old person is not the child they used to be. But nor are they a different person. The self has no existence apart from the habits of mind that go to make it up. It is a process of ever-changing conditions. But it still exists.'

It is the same with rebirth. Rebirth is not the same as reincarnation because there is no unchanging and separate entity that passes from one life to the next. But what does pass to the next life is the self as an ever-changing collection of karmic propensities or choices made in the previous life.'

Very simply, the absence of a soul is seen as a feature of the principle of impermanence.

SN 2, 44.

28. Impermanence

Born into a poor family in Savatthi, Kisa Gotami was at first scorned by her husband's family, but when she brought forth a son she was given respect for the first time.

Then one day whilst playing, her toddler met with an accident and died. As a result Kisa Gotami's mind turned. She went from house to house with the corpse on her hip, asking, 'Please, do you have medicine for my son?'

Everyone who opened the door to her turned her away in disgust, except for one man. He said, 'Go and ask the Buddha.' She found him teaching and pushed forward, interrupting him: 'Give me medicine for my child'. He said 'Very well. Go into the city and find a household that has not seen a death. Take from that house a mustard seed and bring it back to me.'

Joyfully, she called at the first house she came to. 'The Buddha needs a mustard seed to make medicine for my son,' she said. 'If this house has not seen a death, please give me a mustard seed.'

Came the reply, 'The living are few, but the dead are many.' She went to the next door, and the next, always hearing the same answer: 'The living are few but the dead are many.'

Eventually she came to see that it would be like this wherever she went. She also awoke to the suffering of others. Gradually her madness left her. She went to the charnel ground and buried her child. Then she returned to the Buddha, who asked, 'Did you find the mustard seed?' She said, 'The mustard seed has done its work. Please accept me as your disciple.' So Kisa Gotami joined the order of nuns and through mindful attention to her experience, a deepening understanding of impermanence eventually brought her to share the full Enlightenment of a Buddha.

The Buddha saw the same basic delusion that possessed Kisa Gotami in the ordinary person's deep denial of impermanence:

'Here I shall stay in the rains, and there I shall go in the winter, and there in the summer – so much planning, so much confidence!

Preoccupied with children and wealth, you will be carried away by death as a great flood sweeps away a sleeping village.'

The Buddha insisted that impermanence applied everywhere. Even the gods are impermanent. Hell too cannot be for ever. Pain as well as pleasure is impermanent. Most importantly, the path to Enlightenment is possible because change is the nature of what we are.

Thg com 10. Dh 20. SN 4.2

29. How do you know what to believe in?

At one time whilst travelling in the kingdom of Kosala the Buddha arrived at a town of the Kalama tribe. They put it to him: 'Lord, monks and Brahmans who come here all just expound their own tenets while abusing the tenets of others. So how do we know whose view is the truth?'

The Buddha replied, 'You are right to be sceptical about hearsay, or traditional beliefs, or old legends, or holy teaching. But nor should you be satisfied with intellectual conjecture or logical inference or weighing evidence for and against. Not even your own personal inclination, or being impressed by someone, or just assuming 'My teacher knows' can tell you what is the truth.

It is when you know for yourself, from your own experience, 'These doctrines are pernicious, self-evidently reprehensible, condemned by those whose opinion can be trusted, and if taken up and put into practice lead to harm and suffering,' then you should abandon them.

Conversely, when you know for yourself, from your own experience, 'These doctrines are sound and unobjectionable, commended by those I respect, and when put into practice lead to well-being and happiness,' then you should take them up.

Now you know that killing, stealing, sexual misconduct, and lying are harmful. But what leads you into such behaviour? Is it not when the mind is clouded with lust and craving, with hatred, and with delusion? So instead of thinking, saying and doing things that reinforce those negative emotions, you can be sure of being better off cultivating awareness and loving-kindness to all beings, compassion for those in pain, joy for those who are happy, and equanimity to all.

You can then count on at least one of the following assurances:

If the law of karma applies to a life after this one, then it is possible that after death you will be reborn in a heaven realm.

If there is no law of karma, and no heaven or life after death in which you reap the fruits of actions, then here and now in this life you will live happily, free from resentment and anxiety.'

Faith in the Dharma, the Buddha made it clear, is faith in one's own personal experience:

'Well-communicated, immediately apparent, perennial, of the nature of a personal invitation, progressive, to be understood individually by the wise.' *

As well as advising those looking for something to believe, the Buddha challenged plain-speaking cynics, even while he respected their self-reliance.

Taken from the traditional summary of Buddhist faith, the Salutation to the Three Jewels.

A 3.65

30. Self-reliance and mind-training

One morning in the sowing season the Buddha was in a Brahmin village in Magadha and he went out with his begging bowl to where a farmer called Kasibharadvaja was giving his farmhands their lunch. The Buddha stood with them to receive food, but seeing him there the farmer said, 'I plough and sow, then I eat. If you want to eat, you need to work as I do.'

'I too plough and sow, then eat,' said the Buddha. 'I see no ploughing,' responded the farmer, 'where are your oxen, and your ploughshare?'

'The seed I plant is faith. My harness is self-mastery, and my ploughshare is wisdom. Conscience is my guiding pole. Mind is the rope I hold. My goad is mindfulness. Ever watchful over word, deed and thought, I eat only to meet my need. With truth I uproot all weeds. My pair of oxen is the unfaltering effort that leads to the ending of regrets and dismay. This is my ploughing. It bears the fruit of immortality.'

Impressed, the farmer drew out a golden bowl and ladled milk rice into it. But when he respectfully offered it to him, the Buddha refused it.

'I cannot accept a fee or payment in kind for the Dharma.'

'Whom shall I give it to then?'

'Once it has been offered to one who is Awake, it becomes indigestible for anyone else. You must dispose of it where it will do no harm.'

When the farmer went to tip the rice in a stagnant pool, the water hissed and bubbled, as if a hot ploughshare had been plunged into it. Kasibairadvaja's hair stood on end and he prostrated before the Buddha. 'It is as if a lamp has been lit where there was darkness before,' he said. 'Please accept me as your disciple'.

The Buddha was used to teaching capable individuals like the farmer, and often used the language of self-reliance:

'If you care about yourself, tame your own mind. You can't rely on anyone else to do this. No-one can master your mind for you.

The wise guard their thoughts, for they are difficult to become aware of, slippery, and they run where they will. Thoughts well-guarded bring happiness.

Do you always want to be a cowherd who counts other men's cows? Practise the Dharma yourself.

Irrigators channel water, fletchers make arrows true, carpenters straighten timber, and the wise discipline their minds.

Moment by moment remove your impurities, as the smith removes dross from silver.'

SN 1.4. Dh 1, 3, 6, 11, 18

31. Balancing energy: Sona and his guitar

Sona was an unusual youth in that he had hair growing on the soles of his feet. His parents were proud of this distinctive feature, letting it be known that he owed it to his delicate and refined lifestyle. He was not encouraged to put one foot in front of another, so he didn't.

Even King Bimbisara came to hear of him and when he called for a meeting of village representatives he demanded to see the boy. The etiquette of a king examining the soles of the feet of one of his subjects had to be carefully managed. Sona was told to sit cross-legged with his feet upturned, and the king had a good look.

After the meeting, they all adjourned to nearby Vulture's Peak to see and hear the Buddha. They were all duly inspired and uplifted, but when everyone left to return to their everyday lives, Sona insisted on staying, and he became a monk.

Sona found the life of a monk hard; it was not just sitting cross-legged. As well as going out to gather alms, and occasional travel from one village or city to another, they practised walking meditation every afternoon. But Sona had discovered reserves of determination that he did not know were there, and he applied himself to everything the other monks did. However, he was not making progress, and he was starting to think he might be able to do more good with his wealth than with his practice as a monk.

One day the Buddha came by and noticed that one of the walking meditation paths was splattered with blood. He said to some monks nearby, 'This walkway is like a slaughterhouse. Whose is it?' They replied 'Sona's, Lord'.

He went to Sona's lodging and asked him, 'Sona, did you ever play the guitar?

'Yes Lord.'

'So how did you tune it?'

'I used to tighten or loosen the strings until they produced a good sound from the body of the instrument.'

'Well,' the Buddha explained, 'it is the same with your practice of the Dharma. If you are too ardent you will tend to be fanatical, to get wound up and full of yourself. If you are not ardent enough you will of course be sluggish and dull. With both extremes there is a loss of awareness, and thus less control of the mind, and you fall away from the path.'

With this understanding of how to strive, Sona progressed rapidly towards Enlightenment.

The Buddha's 'Middle Way' called for a balancing of energy with patience.

Vin. Mv 5

32. Patience and guarding the mind

The opening verses of the Dhammapada, a compilation of the Buddha's sayings, are associated by the Buddhist tradition with a trivial dispute in the early history of the Sangha.

During the rains retreat at Kosambi in the ninth year of the Buddha's ministry, a senior monk, expert in the ethical discipline of the Sangha, had found in the latrine a water vessel left there by another monk, a teacher of the Dharma. He told him that it was an offence, and the Dharma teacher agreed to acknowledge it. But the Discipline teacher said that if the other had been unaware of the offence, which he said was the case, then there was no offence. However, word got out that the Discipline teacher was unimpressed that the other had not known he was breaking the rules; the Dharma teacher's supporters in turn criticised his accuser: either it was an offence or it wasn't. The Discipline teacher then had the Dharma teacher suspended, who was by then refusing to acknowledge his fault.

The Buddha advised each side to give way. To the Discipline teacher's side he said, 'Don't suspend a sincere practitioner if he has not seen his offence.' To the other he said, 'If your brothers in the Sangha think you have committed an offence just acknowledge it and make amends, even if you do not see it yourself.'

The squabbling monks told the Buddha to leave them to sort it out for themselves. So he did. Eventually the lay-people became so disgusted with them all that they stopped feeding them. The Dharma teacher finally agreed to admit his fault, and the wrangling died down.

The Buddha repeatedly taught his followers to be patient, never to take offence under any circumstances.

'Everything comes from mind. Your experience of yourself and the world is produced by your thoughts. Speak or act from a negative state of mind, and suffering follows as the cartwheel follows the ox. Speak or act from a positive state of mind, and happiness follows like its shadow.

If you keep telling yourself, 'He insulted me, he hurt me, he cheated me, he robbed me' you trap yourself in your own hatred. Stop indulging in such thoughts, and you will free yourself from hatred.

You will never dispel hatred with more hatred. Only love dispels hatred. There is no getting round this law.

Most people do not fully realise that they are going to die at some point. Those who remember their mortality forget their quarrels.'

To maintain patience the Buddha recommended mindfulness above all.

M. 128. Dh 1.

33. Mindfulness

In the town of Sedaka among the Sumbha tribe the Buddha recounted the story of two bamboo acrobats who used to perform together. One day they were rehearsing a show, and as the Master was balancing on the bamboo pole and preparing to take the weight of his assistant, he said 'Now Frying Pan, my dear, the secret here is for you to watch after me and for me to watch after you. If we concentrate on protecting each other we'll be OK.' But as she began her moves Frying Pan replied, 'Master, that can't be right. You watch after yourself, and I'll watch after myself. If each of us looks after ourselves, then together we'll manage the trick safely.'

'Now monks,' said the Buddha, 'to practise mindfulness you must follow young Frying Pan's method. Only by being aware of yourself can you properly watch over others. Then in being fully aware of the needs of others you will look after yourself.'

Mindfulness is the central Buddhist practice. It involves being attentive to the disparate processes that make up moment-by-moment experience. The aim is to interrupt and eliminate habitual patterns of negative thinking, in terms both of the emotional states that inhabit it and the deluded views that maintain it. The practice requires the steady focus of an acrobat, with an awareness that the welfare of others depends upon it.

The Buddha outlined four areas of experience in which to apply mindfulness: the body, feelings, mental states and mind objects. 'This is the direct way to the ending of suffering' he said.

'Sitting upright, cross-legged, and putting aside craving and anxiety, be present with the in-breath, and with the out-breath. Experience the whole body as you breathe. Then reflect on the impermanence of the breath, its fragility, its dependence on so many external and internal conditions. Notice this in yourself and in others. At all times be aware of the body's postures and actions. Don't identify completely with it.

Reflect in the same way on your feelings, whether physical or mental, pleasurable, painful or neutral. Do the same with your mental or emotional state, even as it arises and passes. Distinguish positive emotions or mental states from negative ones. Likewise reflect on the objects of your attention in terms of the teachings.'

'Mindfulness is the way to the immortal, unmindfulness the way to death.'

'The mind is a will-o'-the-wisp. It is good to tame it and then guard it. A tamed and guarded mind is happy.'

The mindful person becomes concentrated and happy.

SN 47. M. 10. Dh 2, 3, 7

34. Meditation: distractions and concentration

An elder called Sangharakkhita was attended by his nephew, who was so unsuccessful in his cultivation of an undistracted mind in meditation that he was considering leaving the Order.

One day while fanning his uncle the nephew started planning his future in his head. He would sell his spare robe and buy a goat which he would breed from until he had enough money to marry. His wife would give birth to a son... At this point the plan turned into a bad daydream. He was taking them in a cart to visit his uncle in the monastery, and arguing with his wife over who carried the child and who drove. As he was grabbing at him the child fell under the wheels. Distraught he hit his wife with the goading stick...

...and absentmindedly hit his uncle over the head with the fan. The elder monk observed mildly, 'You were unable to beat your wife; why have you beaten an old monk?'

Distraction manifests in the form of feelings like anxiety, craving, ill-will, laziness and doubt or indecision.

The Buddha told a Brahman who came to visit him in the Jeta grove of how, in his approach to Enlightenment, he used to deal with a deeper manifestation of these hindrances.

'In spooky forest shrines on holy nights a deer passing, a peacock breaking a twig or the wind in the trees would make my hair stand on end.' But he controlled this fear and dread by not reacting to it in any way: 'When sitting I continued to sit, when walking I did not stop, when standing I did not move.'

Through not indulging negative mental states, they wither, and concentration then arises naturally. The Buddha described to King Ajattasattu the four levels of concentration:

'The first absorption of meditation brings body and mind together like soap powder mixed with water. This unified experience is one of subtle pleasure and happiness. As all thought fades away the second absorption is like a lake fed by a spring bubbling up from below. Then this joy is absorbed into the deep bliss of the third absorption, like lotuses growing under the water. The fourth absorption is beyond pleasure and pain, a vibrant equanimity.'

The result is a trained mind:

'In the past my mind wandered where it liked. Now it is responsive to my will as the rutting elephant answers to its trainer's hook.'

For the Buddha meditation was the cultivation of positive mental states, above all goodwill towards oneself and others.

Dh comm 3. MN 4. DN 2. Dh 23

35. The cultivation of loving-kindness

One year a group of monks went for the rainy season retreat into the forest near Savatthi to meditate. However, at night the monks became frightened by uncanny noises and ghostly apparitions. The local tree deities had been disturbed by the monks' intrusion into their territory and wanted to drive them away.

Eventually the monks went to the Buddha and told him that it seemed as if the forest didn't want them there. The Buddha instructed them in the *metta bhavana,* the cultivation of metta, of boundless loving-kindness.

'If you want to be skilled in cultivating your own well-being and aspire to the ultimate peace that lies beyond self-interest you should firstly be honest, completely upright, soft-spoken, sweet-tempered and modest. Be contented, and undemanding, with few responsibilities, and controlled in your appetites. Be polite but guarded; don't hanker after social distractions. Consider what those you respect would think.

Then contemplate in this way:

May everyone, every living being, be happy and free from worry. May their hearts be free and joyful. However they be judged, inadequate or capable, whatever size or shape, tall, short, fat, thin, leaving no-one out, in this world or any other possible realm of existence, may everyone be happy: the neighbour and the stranger far away; the born and the yet unborn. May no-one betray another or belittle them, or in anger or hatred wish another harm.

Consider the mother who guards her only child with her own life. Cultivate the same attitude of unconditional concern towards everyone you meet, loosening the bonds of the heart to reach out to every living being. Let the heart be open without reservation, to touch every corner of the world with thoughts of loving kindness, looking in every direction for the welfare of beings, all bitterness and resentment gone. In every waking moment of every day, whatever you are doing or not doing, be mindful in this way.

Such a life is the realm of the gods, here and now. Not falling into wrong views, and keeping a straight path of morality, one who uncovers the truth of things, released from all hankerings, will never again have to be reborn.'

Returning to the forest the monks permeated the forest with metta, with thoughts of loving kindness, and they were left in peace. And there they all attained Enlightenment.

With the gradual integration of energies in meditation the mind becomes workable, the Buddha said, like gold, ready to mould itself to the nature of reality.

SN 1. It 1.27 Dh com. 40

36. Measuring attainment: the ten fetters

It was evening in the eastern park near Savatthi and the Buddha was sitting outside the door of his hut after his meditation when King Pasenadi of Kosala approached, prostrated and sat beside him. As he did so various ascetics and wanderers, including a few Jains, were passing by, all unshaven and with long nails, some with coiled hair, others naked. The King got up and went down on one knee to them, announcing his name to them before returning to the Buddha and asking him a question:

'Would you consider that those ascetics were Enlightened?'

The Buddha replied, 'Majesty, because as a lay-follower, you still lead a life devoted to sense pleasures, it is hard for you to tell. In order to judge someone's level of attainment, you need daily contact with them over a long period, and have some insight of your own. All that time you need to be attentive to how they behave and discerning enough to know what to look out for. You have to be able to measure their character and their integrity of conduct, speech and thought. You must also see them in adversity to estimate their fortitude, and enjoy regular discussions to affirm their wisdom.'

'Well, that is fascinating', said the King. 'I should tell you now that I shall soon see those ascetics back in the palace scrubbed and shaven – because they were in fact my local spies.'

Though it is difficult to measure from the outside, the Buddha noted a hierarchy of attainment, according to the number of 'fetters' that are broken.

A Licchavi prince called Mahali once visited the Buddha near Vaisali and asked him what his teaching aimed at. The Buddha outlined four levels of attainment. The first, called 'stream entry' (meaning progress becomes irreversible) is when the first three fetters are broken. These are: self-view – an emotional investment in the idea of a self or soul; doubt in the path or the goal; and dependence on moral codes and religious observances as ends in themselves.

The next level is that of the 'once-returner', who has no more than one further lifetime before full Enlightenment and has weakened the fourth and fifth fetters of sense craving and aversion. The 'non-returner' has eradicated these two fetters and can attain Enlightenment after death from a heaven realm. Finally, someone who is an arahant has broken the five 'higher' fetters. These are: subtle craving for existence in the heaven realms of pure form and no form (manifesting as attachment to higher states of meditation) and subtle levels of conceit, restlessness and delusion.

Ud 6. DN6

37. The nature of Enlightenment

Every so often the circus came to Rajagaha for a week, and one year a boy called Uggasena, son of a financier, fell in love with a beautiful acrobat and joined the circus to be with her. All went well at first, and a child was born. But soon he became aware that his wife despised him - he heard her address the child as 'Son of a cart-driver, a know-nothing'. So he went off and trained as an acrobat himself. In time he became a solo star, and one day he found himself back in his home town.

He set up, and was about to begin his act when the Buddha turned up and the crowd lost interest in his dare-devil feats. He was crestfallen, until a monk came and told him that the Buddha wanted to see him perform. So Uggasena turned 14 somersaults and, as he finished his act, balancing on the swaying bamboo, he heard the Buddha saying,

'Uggasena, drop the past, drop the future, drop the present also. Then you will cross to the further shore, beyond birth and death.'

At this Uggasena attained Enlightenment.

The concentration of an acrobat is necessary for Awakening, but not intellectual ability.

The Buddha gave a simpleton called Culapanthaka a teaching of four lines to repeat to himself. But he kept forgetting the beginning before he got to the end. It was no better with two lines. Even one verse was beyond him. So the Buddha gave him two words to repeat while he swept the meditation hall: 'broom' as he did one side, 'sweep' as he did the other. As his concentration deepened, suddenly a profound insight liberated his mind; the broom and the sweeping disappeared. There was no-one sweeping, and no dust to sweep.

A wanderer called Upasiva, visited the Buddha at the Rock temple near Vaisali and asked him what happened to an Enlightened consciousness. The Buddha said, 'Nirvana is like a flame blowing out. In a flash you have gone out and nothing more can be known about you. But there was not someone there who has disappeared.'

Nirvana is the extinction of all self-concern, of the sense of self that produces and is the result of physical and mental conditioning, but it is not simply nothing:

'There is, monks, a way of being which is beyond the self that is born, made, conditioned. If there were not, there would be no freedom from conditioned existence.' However, once attained there is no nirvana and no samsara. 'Resting nowhere, all fear is gone.'

Dh comm. SN 5. Ud 1. Dh 26

38. The Awakening and death of Bahia

With Enlightenment there is nothing to lose, neither time nor life.

Bahia was a merchant who was shipwrecked and tossed up naked on the shore near Supparaka. He made temporary clothing for himself out of strips of bark, and being taken for a holy man, he took up that role. Eventually he wanted to know if he really was Enlightened, and a spirit who had been his relative appeared to him and told him he was far from it. Bahia asked her where to find someone that was Enlightened. She said, 'One called the Buddha is teaching in the far city of Savatthi.'

So Bahia set out at once, not resting until he came to Savatthi, where he found the Buddha on his alms round, walking mindfully. Bahia threw himself at the Buddha's feet and asked for teaching. The Buddha replied, 'Please wait till I have finished my alms round.' Bahia insisted, 'Who knows when death will take us. Teach me now.' The Buddha again tried to put him off until later, but Bahia was adamant. 'How can we be certain of having a future at all? Teach me.'

The Buddha turned to him. 'Bahia, practise in this way. In the seen only the seen. In the heard only the heard. In the sensed only the sensed. In the known only the known. When for you there is in the seen only the seen, in the heard only the heard, in the sensed only the sensed, in the known only the known, then there will be no room for 'you' there. Just this is the end of suffering.' The Buddha then continued with his alms round. But Bahia was at once fully liberated, fully Enlightened.

Later that day Bahia was trampled by a cow with her calf, and died. Meanwhile the Buddha had finished his alms round and eaten his meal. Returning, he recognised the body of Bahia and told the monks that were with him to take the body and cremate it as a member of the Sangha, and to build a *stupa* * for one who was fully Enlightened.

The Buddha did not mourn Bahia's death.

'The watchful do not long for home. Like wild geese quitting a lake, they leave mundane security behind. Patient as the earth, unshakeable like the gatepost of a city, pure as a still lake, they are free from the rounds of life and death. Wherever they dwell is a place of joy.'

Memorial or reliquary. Known as a 'chorten' in Tibetan, it becomes the pagoda in the far east.

Ud 1. Dh 7

39. Caring for the sick and dying

The Buddha would regularly check up on his disciples when they were together. On one of these rounds he discovered an unpopular monk, Tissa, who had been abandoned when he contracted a disease that brought his body out in boils. These had burst and stained his robes so that he stank. The Buddha boiled water and started to clean him and wash his clothes, before other monks gathered round to finish the job. When he was refreshed, the Buddha taught him:

'The Awakened mind, free from craving, agitation and calculation of good and evil, knows no fear. Look, your body is fragile like a clay pot, but your mind can be strong as a fortress.

The harm from those who hate you is nothing compared to the harm your own mind can do you.'

The good from those who love you is nothing compared to the good your own mind can do you.'

On another occasion the Buddha found a monk with dysentery lying in his own excrement. He asked, 'Is no-one looking after you?'

'No, Lord'.

'Why not?'

'Because I am useless to the Sangha'.

The Buddha and Ananda washed him and put him on a bed. Then the Buddha called the Sangha together and said, 'Monks, you have no parents to look after you. If you do not look after each other, who will? If you would look after me, look after the sick.

A nurse should be perceptive and do the work out of loving-kindness rather than for what they get out of it. He must not be squeamish, and he should be able to offer encouraging talk. The sick monk should co-operate with his nurse, and be cheerful.'

For the Buddha dying was a good opportunity to Awaken. When a dying monk called Vakkali asked to see him, he made his way from Vulture's Peak to the potter's shed where Vakkali was lying. As he entered he said, 'Don't try to get up. I'll sit here, shall I? Now how's it going?'

'Lord it's not looking good for me.'

'I see. I hope in that case that you don't suffer from worry, remorse or regrets?'

'Just that I always wanted to go and see you, Lord. But I've been ill so long.'

'Vakkali, you don't need to see this old carcase. If you see the Dharma you see me. If you see me you see the Dharma.' Before the Buddha left, Vakkali became Enlightened, and being at last fully at peace took his own life.

Vin. Mv. 8.26. Dh 3, 7 Dh com. 41. SN 22

40. Pingiya's faith

Visualising the Buddha was an established practice while he was alive, as the famous dialogue between Pingiya and Bavari attests.

One day the Brahmin Bavari, a master of Vedic mantra, was cursed by a malevolent wanderer who told him that his head would split in seven days. A goddess reassured Bavari that the Buddha could help him. So he sent his disciples to visit the Buddha and ask him about head-splitting. The Buddha said, 'The head is ignorance and it is split by insight, supported by faith, mindfulness, meditation and energy.'

Bavari's disciples then all asked questions of their own.

To a question put by one of them, Udaya, the Buddha replied, 'Recognise the danger in sense objects and give up grasping after them. When sense objects no longer captivate the mind, the flow of compulsive thought comes to an end.' To another, Mogharaja, he said, 'If you are always aware, you will see the emptiness of things. If you give up a fixed and special identity for yourself, you give yourself a way to go beyond death.'

When the eldest of the disciples, Pingiya, returned, he announced to Bavari,

'I will sing you the praises of the Way to the Beyond. It is like a bird flying up from the dry scrub to the forest fruit trees. I too have flown the murk of fixed views. Like a swan I have arrived at a great lake.

Until now all I heard was 'This is how things must always be because it is laid down by our ancient holy traditions,' thereby setting off endless speculation. But this man, Gotama the Buddha, has brought light into this obscurity. His wisdom is universal, his understanding reaches to the world's end. His teaching is the way things are; it is immediately present, dissolving craving harmlessly. It is unlike anything else in the world.'

'So then,' asked Bavari, 'why do you not live closer to him?'

'Because I am never apart from Gotama the Buddha, even here. Because with constant mindful attention I am able to see him in my mind as clearly as with my eyes. I cannot now lose the teaching: the powers of faith and joy, of conceptual understanding and intuitive awareness sustain it in my mind.

I am old and physically I cannot follow him, but the power of thought carries me to him. Yes, I shall go there, beyond this uncertain world. There are no more doubts. Look, here is a mind released.'

However, not all the Buddha's disciples revered him. There was one who thought he could do a better job himself.

SN 5.

41. Devadatta: the great betrayer

The story of the schismatic Devadatta appears to be embellished with legendary material in order to demonise him and create a powerful myth of betrayal. In fact, followers of his sect could be found in India a thousand years later.

The historical basis of the first split in the Sangha was Devadatta's recommendation of tighter rules for the Order: that the monks should eat no meat; that they should just beg for food, and never accept invitations to meals; that they should not accept robes made for them, but wear genuine rags; that they should always live in the wild, never indoors. However, the Buddha insisted that monks should have the option to be more or less strict about these issues.

Devadatta was the Buddha's cousin and the legend has it that he was so accomplished in meditation that he developed supernormal powers. But he also craved fame and power. First he won the favour of Prince Ajatasattu, son of King Bimbisara. Then in front of the whole Sangha he suggested to the Buddha that being now quite old the Buddha should resign the leadership of the Sangha to him. The Buddha refused, and the attempt to wrest control of the Sangha away from the Buddha immediately caused Devadatta to lose his supernormal powers.

The Buddha had Devadatta denounced in Rajagaha as no longer a member of the Sangha. Meanwhile Devadatta advised Ajatasattu to kill his father while he himself would kill the Buddha. Ajatasattu was discovered suspiciously armed in King Bimbisara's palace and admitted to his father that he was bent on killing him. But his father simply passed the kingdom over to him anyway.

For his part Devadatta sent an assassin to kill the Buddha, trying to cover his tracks by having the assassin himself killed, and those killers killed themselves. But none were able to carry out their orders and they all became the Buddha's disciples. Next he pushed a boulder down from Vulture's Peak onto the path where the Buddha was walking. It missed but a splinter of rock gashed the Buddha's foot.

Finally Devadatta had a rogue elephant released into the road when the Buddha came by. As it charged the Buddha, he enveloped it with loving-kindness, which stopped it in its tracks. This very public attempt on the Buddha's life turned the people against Devadatta. His followers went back to the Buddha, and he himself died of apoplexy.

King Ajatasattu imprisoned his father, the Buddha's old friend, and had him starved to death. But even he would not be able to resist the Buddha's compassion.

Vin. Cv. 7:2-4. S. 3:14-15

42. The fruits of the Buddhist life

One night in Rajagaha, the new King Ajatasattu was on the roof of his palace with his ministers, enjoying the full moon: 'This is an auspicious night!' he said. 'A night to visit a holy man, one who may bring peace to my heart.'

His ministers suggested various great teachers. One spoke of Makkhali Gosala, the fatalist, another suggested Nigantha, the founder of Jainism, and someone else mentioned Ajita Kesambala the materialist. The king was silent. Then he turned to Jivaka, his physician. 'Well?'

'Your Majesty, the Buddha is staying in my mango grove with 1200 monks.'

'Good! Jivaka, call for my elephants.'

Torchbearers lit the way for their retinue of 500 elephants as they tramped out of the city gates. But as the noise of the city faded behind them, and they neared the mango grove, a deadly chill gripped the King's heart.

' Jivaka, this is not a trap is it? There cannot be 1200 men here. There is no sound. Do not betray me, Jivaka.'

'Be at peace, great king. See, the lamps.'

They dismounted. 'But where is the Buddha?' whispered Ajatasattu.

'There, great king, look.'

Twelve hundred monks sat still, like a smooth lake. The king sighed:

'If only my son might have such peace as this.'

Then he approached the Buddha and bowed. 'I have a question, Lord.' 'Go on.' 'It is this. What are the fruits of the monk's life to be found here and now?'

The Buddha replied: 'First, Your Majesty, a morally scrupulous life gives you a positive outlook. Then by guarding the senses you do not get pulled this way and that by compulsive thoughts. And living a simple life, you are content.

Next, meditation frees the mind from anxiety, craving, ill-will, idleness and debilitating doubt. This feels like being freed from debt, or prison or slavery. It is like recovering from sickness. It is like one lost in a desert who arrives at length at a village.

Finally you direct the mind to knowing and seeing the true nature of body and mind. You see and know the origin and ending of suffering. This is freedom.

These are the fruits of the monk's life, Your Majesty, to be found here and now.'

Regretting all that he had lost in getting all he wanted Ajatasattu confessed his wrongdoing in killing his father. And with his mind at peace he departed.

Twenty years later, Ajatasattu's son murdered him in turn. As for the Buddha, in this time of political instability his own life was now nearing its end.

DN 2

43. The Buddha's farewell to life

The Buddha's final years provided a sober affirmation of his teaching on impermanence. His son, Rahula, and his two chief disciples, Sariputta and Moggallana, had already died, as had his old friend King Pasenadi. But in the midst of death, the Buddha delighted in life.

When Ambapali the courtesan heard that the Buddha was staying in her park near Vaisali, she drove out in her finest carriage to call on him. After listening to his teaching, she invited him and his monks to take a meal from her the next day; the Buddha consented. As she was returning, she met a group of smart young men of the Licchavi tribe, and rode up to them, axle to axle.

She told them that she had beaten them to the honour of feeding the city's illustrious guest, and they snapped their fingers, 'The mango-girl has stolen a march on us! She's outfoxed us!' As they rode up to greet him the Buddha remarked, 'If you have never had a vision of the Heaven of the Thirty-Three Gods, just look at this band of gallants.' The next day the Sangha went to Ambapali's residence, where she made a gift to the Buddha of her city park.

From Vaisali the Buddha went with Ananda on retreat to Beluva for the rainy season. There he felt the first pangs of death, which he suppressed by force of will so that he could take proper leave of the Sangha. One day, as he sat on the outside step of his dwelling Ananda told him that he was reassured by the thought that his teacher would not pass away without some final pronouncement to the Order.

'But what does the Order expect of me? I don't keep back esoteric teachings. I have no 'teacher's closed fist'. I am not 'in charge' of the Order for that matter. Ananda, I am eighty years old, worn out. I keep going like a patched up old cart. It is only when I can sit in meditative concentration that I am comfortable. Each of you should live as an island unto yourself, with the Dharma as your refuge, with mindfulness, and no other refuge than that.'

After the rains the Buddha returned to Vaisali for the last time. Before leaving he sat with Ananda and gazed at the city in admiration from one of its beauty spots, the Capala shrine. He knew that he would not see it again.

It was at this time that news came of the invasion and massacre of the Buddha's tribe, the Sakyans, by King Pasenadi's son.

DN 16

44. The passing of the Buddha

Travelling from one settlement to another, the ailing Buddha gave the same discourse wherever he went, on ethics, meditation, wisdom and release. At Pava he took his last meal provided by Cunda the goldsmith, after which he was seized with severe diarrhoea. As they set off again, he told Ananda to make sure that Cunda should feel no remorse at having brought on his final bout of sickness. Then they crossed the river to the Mallans' sal tree grove at the turn into Kusinara, where the Buddha finally lay down between two trees that bloomed out of season, dropping blossoms onto his body.

Ananda withdrew to his lodging, where he stood leaning against the door, weeping, 'I have still so much to learn, and my teacher who was so kind is passing away.' Hearing of this the Buddha called for him and said, 'Ananda, do not weep. Whatever is born must die. This is how things are. You have looked after me long and unstintingly, and with great kindness. Devote yourself now to your practice and soon you will be free of anguish.'

The Buddha then turned to the assembly of monks who were gathering and spoke in praise of Ananda's virtues, his skill with people, his tact, his charm and friendliness.

Ananda was sent to tell the local people what was happening, and when they started to arrive he shepherded them in groups to see the Buddha. Amongst them was a wanderer called Subhadda who had turned up to question the Buddha. Ananda tried to put Subhadda off but the Buddha insisted on seeing him, and he became the last of the Buddha's direct disciples.

There were other items of business that he insisted on dealing with: his old charioteer Channa, was not to be spoken to until he confessed to his ungovernable temper. He also told Ananda that the minor rules of the Order could be dropped. Then he reassured him: 'Do not imagine that my teaching will cease when I am gone. The Dharma shall be your teacher.'

Finally he turned to the assembled monks: 'If you have any question or concern in your mind about my teaching, speak now, so that when I am gone you don't regret not raising the issue with me in person. If you are shy, ask a friend to speak for you.' No-one spoke. Then came his last words,

'All conditioned things are liable to decay. With mindfulness, strive.'

The Buddha entered into meditative concentration and finally passed away. Thus he attained parinirvana, Enlightenment with no longer a foot in the world.

DN 16

45. The Buddha's funeral and the first Council

The morning after the Buddha's parinirvana Ananda went to inform the local people of the Buddha's passing, and they came with perfume, wreaths, tents and musicians to spend the day celebrating the Buddha's life and worshipping his body with dance and song. They carried on for a week and then brought the body into Kusinara, where even the sewers and rubbish heaps were covered in coral tree flowers.

Ananda passed on the Buddha's instruction that the body of a Buddha be treated like that of a great king, but that the monks should not concern themselves with the funeral arrangements, and just get on with their practice.

The Buddha's chief disciple, Mahakassapa, was on the road from Pava with 500 monks when a man wearing a coral tree flower told them of their master's passing. Weeping and wailing broke out amidst the monks, though one of them was heard to announce 'We are well rid of the Buddha with his 'do this' and 'do that' – now we can do as we like.'

Only when Mahakassapa had arrived and paid his respects was the funeral pyre lit and the body burned. The tribes and rulers who had known the Buddha in his life then vied for his relics. These were divided into eight parts and stupas built over them in the cities of the Ganges where he had taught and amidst the peoples from whom he had begged for alms.

A few weeks after the parinirvana, Mahakassapa called a council of senior monks at Rajagaha. However, one of them, Ananda, was not yet an arahant. But all night he meditated, and at dawn when he lay down, before his head touched the pillow and after his feet had left the ground, he attained liberation.

The Council agreed on a collection of suttas or discourses to be memorised and passed down orally. It also agreed on a list of rules of the Order, though Ananda was censured for not asking the Buddha which of the rules he considered minor and therefore could be dropped.

Not long after, Mahakassapa again criticised Ananda, together with his undisciplined followers '...who do not guard the gates of their senses, who eat immoderately, and are uncommitted to their practice. This boy does not know his own limits.' 'Let us have less of the boy, Mahakassapa,' replied Ananda, 'I have white hairs on my head.'

By the time of the second council, a hundred years later, a split had occurred within the Sangha. Out of this split emerged bold new ways of presenting the Dharma.

DN 16. Vin Cv 11

46. The Lotus Sutra

While the Pali suttas provide historians with most of what they know of the political events and social life of the Buddha's time, the Mahayana sutras, originally written in Sanskrit, go beyond history, and even conventional notions of time and space.

The Lotus Sutra emerged in the 1st century AD and is venerated throughout East Asia. Like other Mahayana works it aims to clarify the Buddhist goal as not just to become Enlightened, but to become a Buddha, one who shows the way for others. Its ideal Buddhist is not an arahant but a Bodhisattva, one whose goal is to become Enlightened for the sake of all beings. Only a Buddha can Awaken; yet all beings share in this capacity - they all have this 'Buddha-nature'.

The sutra begins conventionally, with Ananda and the Buddha Sakyamuni, 'the sage of the Sakyans' on Vulture's Peak. But they also inhabit a visionary world.

While the Buddha meditated, surrounded by 12,000 arahants, 80,000 bodhisattvas, and thousands of gods, a ray of light from between his eyebrows illumined the universe, revealing world systems in all directions, in each of which Buddhas were teaching. Maitreya, who is to be the next Buddha in this world, asked 'What does this mean?' Manjusri, the bodhisattva of wisdom, replied, 'the Buddha is about to preach the White Lotus Sutra.'

The Buddha declared that even when ultimate truth is out of reach, every little positive action, word or thought takes us towards it.

'Even if they do not encounter the teaching of the Buddha, individuals who are ethical and kind have all attained the Buddha way.'

He then expounded the Mahayana principle of 'skilful means': giving people what they need to progress towards what they cannot understand. He did this through the parable of the burning house. 'Imagine', said the Buddha, 'a wealthy man with dozens of children, all living in a rambling, old, decaying house. When a fire breaks out he is unable to persuade the children of the danger and to break off from their playing. So he tells them that he has different kinds of toy carts waiting for them outside, and the children rush out and are safe. And when they ask for their toys their father gives them all magnificent carriages. I am that rich man', the Buddha explained, 'the burning house is this world, the children are the people of this world engrossed in their pleasures and hatreds, and the different carts are the different levels of teaching that those people need.'

This is just the first of a number of parables in the sutra.

LS

47. The Lotus Sutra: parables and prophecies

Much of the Lotus Sutra is about the White Lotus Sutra, how it must be recited and honoured and taught, with dire warnings against speaking ill of it. But where the sutra itself begins and ends remains elusive. In this way the structure of the sutra illustrates how the Buddha's teachings prepare us for a truth that cannot be grasped or approached directly. The sutra's parables do the same.

The Buddha told a parable about a man who left home and lived in destitution while his father became fabulously rich. After many years he arrived in the town where his father now lived looking for work, but did not recognise the old man. Seeing him, his father gave him work shovelling muck, and a hovel to sleep in near the palace. Over the years the son got used to going in and out of the palace, and eventually was made steward of all the old man's property. Gradually he got used to handling money and giving orders until finally the old man told him that he was in fact his son and heir. Likewise, the Buddha explained, we all come into our inconceivably rich spiritual inheritance by slow degrees.

The Buddha's next parable was of a rain cloud, which rains equally on all the different plants and trees. The same rain enables them to grow and flourish each in their own individual way. The Buddha is the rain cloud and his Dharma falls on all beings equally, but nourishing each in the way that suits their individual needs.

Then the Buddha prophesied that his historical disciples would all become Buddhas, including his betrayer Devadatta, who he said had been his own teacher in a past life. Delighted, the assembled arahants agreed that they each felt like a man who has endured great hardship and want, not realising that he had a precious jewel sewn into his robe.

Finally a colossal jewelled stupa sprang from the earth and towered into the sky. From it the thunderous voice of a previous Buddha, called Abundant Treasures, announced, 'Excellent Sakyamuni! You are well able to preach the White Lotus Sutra.' The Buddha Sakyamuni explained that the ancient Buddha had made a vow to appear whenever the White Lotus Sutra was taught. Then the door of the stupa opened, and Sakyamuni approached and sat next to Abundant Treasures. Sakyamuni revealed that he himself had been teaching bodhisattvas for incalculable ages in many different world systems. He only appeared to be born and die so that people would listen to a message that is, in reality, always present.

WLS

48. The Happy Land Sutra

Written down in the 2nd century, the larger Sukhavativyuha Sutra or Happy Land Sutra, inspired the 'Pure Land' schools of China and Japan that are based on reciting the name of the Buddha Amitabha.

At one time Ananda asked the historical Buddha if he were contemplating the Buddhas of the past. The Buddha confirmed that this was the case and went on to introduce the monk called Dharmakara who would become the Buddha Amitabha.

The Buddha said to Ananda, 'In a time so long ago that it is beyond the power of thought to reckon, there was a moment at which a Buddha of ancient times, Dipankara, took his first step in the world. After his teaching was lost another Buddha rediscovered the Path, and in the following age another. The eightieth Buddha after Dipankara was Lokesvararaja, who had a disciple of many wonderful qualities, called Dharmakara.

And on a certain occasion Dharmakara knelt before Lokesvararaja and declared:

'The Dharma is deep, wide and subtle. The best of Buddhas is unfathomable, like the ocean. Boundlessly luminous, he illumines all regions. May I too become a Buddha, a master of the Dharma, so as to deliver all beings from old age and death.

And I undertake to make this noblest of wishes into my primary duty by the practice of giving, ethics, patience, energy, meditation and concentration.

To attain their wisdom I shall ceaselessly worship the incomparable Buddhas, numberless like the sands of the Ganges.

My mastery shall be to illumine numberless worlds, which shall unceasingly manifest my aspiration.

Abiding even in the Avici hell, in the deepest suffering, may I endure it as long as it may last without forgetting my aspiration for a moment.'

Then Dharmakara asked Lokesvararaja, 'Please teach me all the excellent qualities of the Pure Lands of all the unnumbered Buddhas in unnumbered universes, so that we may then put them all into practical effect.' So for a hundred million years, Lokesvararaja taught him, out of compassion for beings, whether human, divine or demonic; and afterwards, while universes came and went Dharmakara meditated upon the perfected qualities of Pure Buddha Lands, concentrating them into one Pure Land. Then he bowed down in worship at the feet of Lokesvararaja, who said,

'Inspire the assembly of monks with your vows to create the perfect Buddha Land. Give future Bodhisattvas, those who wish to bring all beings to awakening, directions for their quest.'

In reply Dharmakara gave voice to his aspiration, describing the world he would bring about through the power of his compassion.

LSV

49. Amitabha's vows

The vision of a paradisal world of luminous colour that follows does not describe the final goal, but rather an ideal mythical world in which to awaken to the nature of reality.

Dharmakara, the future Buddha Amitabha, staked his attainment of Enlightenment on his ability, when he did attain it, to establish a perfect Pure Land. He announced to the Buddha,

'Lord, none in my Buddha world shall suffer pain, hatred, fear, jealousy or craving, like animals or hell-beings.

   Or let me not attain the highest wisdom.

All shall be empowered with miraculous mastery of their own mind, with supreme supersensory perception, and with the strength of body of the diamond thunderbolt of Narayana.

   Or let me not attain.

None shall have the idea of possessing anything, even their own body, all shall have clear knowledge of the Dharma, and the word 'fault' shall not exist in that world.

   Or let me not attain.

I shall appear to beings in other worlds, at the time of their death, to comfort them, when in life they have cultivated the highest wisdom and have meditated on me.

   Or let me not attain.

Anyone anywhere who hears my Buddha name and conceives a pure aspiration to be born in my Pure Land, even if they repeat that aspiration just ten times, shall be reborn in my Pure Land.

   Or let me not attain.

Those born in my Pure Land shall have to be reborn only once more before attaining nirvana, except for those who undertake the higher aspiration of the Bodhisattva and hold back their own Enlightenment in order to help others.

    Or let me not attain.

Corals, amber, and red pearls, whatever beauty arises in the minds of beings in my Pure Land shall appear there before them. And none shall know the bounds of the beauty of this land, its air perfumed with jewel-like flowers, descending from clouds sounding with sweet music.

    Or let me not attain.'

Dharmakara concluded with these verses:

'The lord of infinite light has brought peace to the heart, he has quieted the fire in the walk of hell. He is the treasure of all who suffer.

    May I too be such a guide for all beings.

And if my vow is fulfilled, may the thousand worlds tremble and a rain of flowers fall upon the gods.'

Then the earth trembled, blossoms fell from the sky, and there was a voice saying, 'You will be a Buddha for the world.'

'In this way,' said the Buddha to Ananda, 'was Dharmakara established in the attainment of the true vow.'

SVS

50. The Diamond Sutra

As the sutras extolling the path of compassion were appearing, another radically different approach was being expressed in very different ways.

Chan Buddhism in China, or in Japanese Zen, specialises in meditation and draws its literary inspiration from the extensive family of Mahayana sutras called the Perfection of Wisdom, which emerged from the 1st century BC. The most celebrated of these is the Diamond Sutra, dating from the 4th century, so called because its wisdom cuts like a diamond through all fixed ideas about reality, particularly Buddhist ones. In the famous Zen image, the whole of Buddhism is but a finger pointing at the moon; in order to see the moon we must look beyond the finger.

There is therefore no Buddhist creed or 'Holy Book', no fixed deposit of truth. All wisdom must be transcended in a direct experience of sunyata, the 'emptiness' of anything the mind grasps at or depends upon.

The Diamond Sutra begins conventionally, with the Buddha going begging for food in Sravasti and returning to the Jeta grove to meditate, whereupon he engages in a densely paradoxical debate with his disciple Subhuti.

The Buddha said, 'A Bodhisattva must resolve to guide all beings to nirvana whilst seeing that in reality no being exists. Moreover, a Bodhisattva's compassion helps people without any *idea* of helping, or even any idea of people to help. He or she gives with no concept or even *perception* of giving. Indeed, no amount of doing good in the world is as meritorious as teaching just one verse of the Dharma with no idea of making merit by it.'

The Buddha asked: 'Subhuti, have I ever taught or demonstrated any truth whatsoever?' 'No, Lord', said Subhuti, 'nor have I, as an Enlightened being, attained to anything.' 'And is any teaching passed on from one mind to another?' said the Buddha. 'No Lord,' said Subhuti. 'The transmission is real because it is empty.' The Buddha went on, 'A Bodhisattva resolves to create a Pure Land only by not thinking of creating a Pure Land. Moreover, the perfection of patience is no patience, because in it there is no idea of a self that might be hurt.'

The Buddha then named this teaching: 'the wisdom which has gone beyond'; and the teacher of it the Tathagatha, one who has not gone anywhere or come from anywhere, concluding,

> 'As stars, a trick of the light, or a flickering lamp,
>
> A magic show, a dewdrop or a bubble,
>
> A dream, or lightning, clouds forming and reforming,
>
> So should we regard all conditioned things.'

DS

Also in this series

The 100-Minute Bible
ISBN 97809551324-0-7
and 97809556695-5-2

The 100-Minute Torah
ISBN 97809556695-2-1

The 100 Minute Qur'an
ISBN 97809556695-4-5

www.the100-minutepress.com